The Little Book of
Weddings

The Little Book of Weddings
An Anthology

Edited by Will Balliett

A Balliett & Fitzgerald Book

THE ATLANTIC MONTHLY PRESS
NEW YORK

DESIGN BY SUSAN CANAVAN

Published simultaneously in Canada
Printed in the United States of America

First edition

Library of Congress Cataloging-in-Publication Data

The little book of weddings: an anthology / edited by Will Balliett.
     p.   cm.
  "A Balliett & Fitzgerald Book"
  ISBN 0-87113-629-5
  1. Weddings—Literary collections.   I. Balliett, Will.
PN6071.W4L58 1996
808.8'0355—dc20   95-39292

The Atlantic Monthly Press
841 Broadway
New York, NY 10003

10 9 8 7 6 5 4 3 2 1

contents

introduction

After I got married, I would find myself announcing "The reason I never enjoyed a wedding before was that none of them was mine." The one bit of wisdom this blissfully selfish comment implies is that weddings are not necessarily uniformly joyous occasions, even when the bride and groom are having a transcendent time. Which is good news for this collection. Because from an editorial standpoint, the only good wedding is a bad wedding. Gauche excess, tearful debauch and silent heartbreak make for much more entertaining reading than the happy memories of a boringly blissful bride and groom (except, of course, when the bride and groom are Charles and Di observed in hindsight; see page 55).

Accordingly, *The Little Book of Weddings* has its share of tales told by and about anyone but the bride and groom, from their once (and future) lovers to the hysterical parents. When the bride and groom *do* become the focus, events can become even more surreal. How about eloping in the midst of wild buffalo, arranging to have P. T. Barnum as your wedding planner, or marrying your cousin at your uncle's suggestion? These occasions do not necessarily turn out tragically. But they *are* different from most. Which, come to think of it, may be a hidden bonus to this collection.

The Little Book of Weddings allows you to get all your traumatic, difficult and "different" weddings out of the way without having to be a member of the wedding party or even get out of bed for that matter. There's also lively spectacle, as well as some inspiring party ideas and a few happy endings (with no embarrassment spared along the way, of course). But what this book practically guarantees is that when you decide to have a wedding of your own, you will have paid your dues—vicariously at least—and gained a better chance of going the boringly blissful route. To make doubly sure, avoid having anyone write about it.—W.B.

Madame Bovary

(an excerpt)

Gustave Flaubert

In addition to a lavish bacchanal (the cake alone makes Martha Stewart look like an amateur), Flaubert depicts the many different emotional currents sweeping the party along, from the giddy groom to Emma's grieving father.

Emma would have preferred to be married at midnight, by torchlight, but this idea seemed senseless to her father. So there was a traditional wedding with forty-three guests who remained at table for sixteen hours, began the celebration all over again the next day and kept it up more or less for several days afterward.

The guests arrived early in a variety of vehicles: carryalls, two-wheeled charabancs, old gigs without tops, vans with leather curtains; and the young men from the nearby villages came in carts, standing beside each other in rows and gripping the rails to keep from falling as they bumped along behind the trotting horses. They came from twenty-five miles around, from Goderville, Normanville and Cany. All the relatives of both families had been invited; quarrels between friends had been patched up; letters had been written to acquaintances who had long since dropped out of sight.

Now and then the crack of a whip would be heard behind the hedge; soon afterward the gate would open and a carryall would roll in. It would go on at a gallop as far as the front steps, then stop short and begin discharging its passengers, who would climb out on all sides, rubbing their knees and stretching their arms. The ladies wore bonnets and city-style dresses, with gold watch chains, tippets whose ends were crossed and tucked into their belts, or small colored scarves pinned at the back and leaving the neck bare. The boys, dressed exactly like their papas, looked uncomfortable in their new clothes (many of them, in fact, were wearing boots for the first time in their lives), and beside them there was often some tall, red-faced girl of fourteen or fifteen, probably their cousin or older sister, standing speechless and bewildered in her white First Communion dress lengthened for the occasion, her hair sticky with rose pomade, terribly worried about soiling her gloves. Since there were not enough stablemen to unharness all the vehicles, the men rolled up their sleeves and did it themselves. According to their social status, they wore tail coats, frock coats, long jackets or short jackets. The tail coats were fine garments, each one held in high esteem by an entire family and taken out of the closet only on great occasions; the frock coats had full skirts that billowed in the wind, cylindrical collars and pockets as wide as bags; the long jackets, made of coarse woolen cloth, were in most cases worn with a cap whose visor was trimmed with brass; the short jackets had two buttons in back, set close together like a pair of eyes, and stubby tails which looked as though they had been cut from a single block by a carpenter's ax. A few guests (these, of course, would sit at the foot of the table) wore dress smocks; that is, smocks with collars turned down over the shoulders, pleated backs and stitched belts worn very low.

And the shirts bulged out like breastplates! Every man was freshly shorn, ears stuck out sharply from every head, every face was closely shaven. Some of the men, having gotten up before dawn, had not been able to see clearly when they shaved; as a result, they had diagonal gashes under their noses, or patches of skin as wide as a three-franc coin sliced from their jaws. These cuts had been inflamed by the wind during the journey, so that the big, beaming white faces were mottled with red spots.

Since the town hall was only a little more than a mile from the farm, the entire party went there on foot and returned the same way after the church ceremony. At first the procession was like a single brightly colored scarf undulating across the countryside along the narrow path that wound through the green grain, but it soon began to stretch out thin and break up into separate groups which lingered along the way to talk. The fiddler walked in front with his violin, which was adorned with ribbons hanging from its scroll; then came the bride and groom with their relatives behind them; the other guests followed in a disorderly band, and the children dallied behind, amusing themselves by pulling the bellflowers from among the oat stalks, or frolicking with each other, out of sight of their parents. Emma's dress, too long, trailed on the ground a little; she would stop now and then to pull it up and daintily pick off the coarse blades of grass and thistle spikes with her gloved fingers while Charles stood by empty-handed, waiting for her to finish. Monsieur Rouault, wearing a new silk hat and a black tail coat whose sleeves hung down to his fingertips, had given his arm to the elder Madame Bovary. As for the elder Monsieur Bovary, who, basically despising all those people, had come wearing merely a long single-breasted coat of military cut, he was busy addressing barroom gallantries to a blond young peasant girl who nodded and blushed, not knowing what to answer. The other members of the wedding party were discussing business matters or playing tricks behind each other's backs, working themselves up in advance for the merriment that was to come. And, if they listened, they could hear the fiddler, who continued to scrape his instrument as he walked across the fields. Whenever he noticed that the others were lagging far behind him, he would stop to catch his breath, carefully rub his bow with rosin to make the strings squeak better, then set off again, bobbing the neck of his violin up and down to keep time. His music frightened away all the birds within a wide radius.

The table had been set up in the cart shed. On it were four sirloin roasts, six chicken fricassees, a veal casserole, three legs of mutton and, in the center, a beautiful roast suckling pig flanked by four large sausages made of chitterlings and sorrel. At the corners stood decanters of brandy. The cider was foaming up around the corks and every glass had been filled to the brim with wine. Big dishes of yellow custard, on whose smooth surface the newlyweds' initials had been inscribed in arabesques of sugar-coated almonds, quivered whenever the table was given the slightest knock. The pies and nougat had been ordered from a confectioner in Yvetot. Since he had just opened up shop in the district he had done his best to make a good impression, and when it was time for dessert he personally carried in a wedding cake which brought forth a chorus of exclamations. Its base was a square of blue cardboard representing a temple with porticos and colonnades, adorned on all sides with stucco statuettes standing in niches studded with gilded paper stars. The second tier consisted of a fortified castle tower made of spongecake, surrounded by smaller fortifications of angelica, almonds, raisins and sections of orange. And finally, on the top layer, which was a green meadow with rocks, jelly lakes and hazelnut-shell boats, a little cupid was swinging in a chocolate swing whose two uprights were tipped with real rosebuds.

The eating went on till nightfall. When some of the guests became tired of sitting down, they would take a stroll through the barnyards or go into a barn and play a game of corkpenny, then they would return to the table. Toward the end, a few people fell asleep and snored. But everything came to life again when the coffee was served: there were songs and feats of strength; the men carried heavy weights, put their heads under their arms while holding their thumbs on the table, tried to raise carts on their shoulders, told spicy stories, kissed the ladies. Later in the evening, when it was time to leave, the horses, stuffed to the nostrils with oats, were placed between the shafts only with great difficulty; they kicked, reared and broke their harnesses while their masters cursed or laughed; and all night long, in the moonlight on the country roads, there were runaway carryalls bouncing along ditches at a wild gallop, leaping over piles of stones and sideswiping embankments, with women leaning out, trying to catch hold of the reins.

Those who stayed behind at Les Bertaux spent the night drinking in the kitchen. The children went to sleep under the benches.

The bride had begged her father to see to it that she was spared the usual practical jokes. However, one of their cousins, a fishmonger (who had brought a pair of soles as a wedding gift), was about to squirt water from his mouth through the keyhole when Monsieur Rouault came along just in time to stop him, explaining that the dignity of his son-in-law's position forbade such unseemly pranks. The cousin gave in to him with extreme reluctance. He inwardly accused Rouault of snobbishness and went off to a corner to join four or five other guests who had, by chance, been given inferior cuts of meat at the table several times in succession and therefore felt that they too had been badly treated; they all whispered malicious remarks about their host and, in veiled language, expressed hopes for his ruin.

The elder Madame Bovary had not opened her mouth all day. She had not been consulted about her daughter-in-law's wedding dress or the arrangements for the celebration; she retired early. Instead of going with her, her husband sent to Saint-Victor for cigars and stayed up till dawn, smoking and drinking hot toddies made with kirsch, a mixture that was new to the other guests; it made him feel that they held him in even greater esteem.

Charles was not jocular by nature, and his conversation during the festivities had not been sparkling. He made feeble replies to the witticisms, puns, equivocal remarks, compliments and broad jokes which everyone felt duty-bound to toss at him all through the meal.

The next day, however, he seemed a different man. It was he who acted as though he had lost his virginity during the night, while the bride's behavior revealed nothing whatever. Even the shrewdest observers were puzzled, and they carefully scrutinized her whenever she came near. But Charles hid nothing. He called her "my wife," used the intimate form of address when he spoke to her, kept asking everyone where she was and looking for her everywhere, and often took her out into the yard, where he could be seen in the distance, through the trees, walking with his arm around her waist, leaning over her and rumpling with his head the tucker she was wearing over her bodice.

The bride and groom left two days after the wedding: because of his patients, Charles could stay no longer. Monsieur Rouault had them taken back in his carryall and went with them as far as Vassonville. There he gave his daughter one last kiss, got out and began walking back toward Les Bertaux. He turned around after taking a hundred steps or so, and as he watched the carryall moving away from him, its wheels spinning in the dust, he heaved a deep sigh. He recalled his own wedding, his own youth, his wife's first pregnancy; he, too, had been happy the day he took her from her father's house to his own. She had ridden behind him on his horse as it trotted through the snow, for it had been close to Christmas and the fields were white; she had held onto him with one arm while her basket hung from the other; she was wearing the traditional headdress of the Caux region, and the long lace streamers fluttered in the wind, occasionally blowing across his mouth. Each time he looked around he saw her rosy little face pressed up against his shoulder, smiling silently at him from beneath the gold plaque of her bonnet. From time to time she would warm her fingers by putting them inside his coat. It was all so long ago! Their son would now be thirty if he were still alive! He looked back again and saw nothing on the road. He felt desolate and dreary, like an empty, deserted house, and as tender memories and gloomy thoughts mingled in his mind, which was still beclouded by the vapors of the feast, he had a momentary impulse to head toward the church. Since he was afraid the sight of it might make him even sadder, however, he went straight home.

Plaza Suite

(an excerpt from act III of the play)

Neil Simon

Here are a father and mother who would just like to get their daughter out of the hotel bathroom in which she's locked herself, with a ballroom full of guests waiting to see her married. Roy and Norma's repartee might explain her panic.

ROY   Is she in there?

NORMA   She's in there! She's in there! *(Hobbling to the far side of the bed and sitting down on the edge)* Where am I going to get another pair of stockings now? How am I going to go to the wedding with torn stockings?

ROY   *(Crossing to the bathroom)* If she doesn't show up, who's going to look at you? *(He kneels at the door and looks through the keyhole)* There she is. Sitting there and crying.

NORMA   I *told* you she was in there . . . The only one in my family to have a daughter married in the Plaza and I have torn stockings.

ROY   *(He is on his knees, his eye to the keyhole)* Mimsey, I can see you . . . Do you hear me? . . . Don't turn away from me when I'm talking to you.

NORMA   Maybe I can run across to Bergdorf's. They have nice stockings.
    (Crosses to her purse on the bureau in the bedroom and looks through it)

ROY   *(Still through the keyhole)* Do you want me to break down the door, Mimsey, is that what you want? Because that's what I'm doing if you're not out of there in five seconds . . . Stop crying on your dress. Use the towel!

NORMA   *(Crossing to* ROY *at the door)* I don't have any money. Give me four dollars, I'll be back in ten minutes.

ROY   *(Gets up and moves below the bed)* In ten minutes she'll be a married woman, because I've had enough of this nonsense. *(Yells in)* All right, Mimsey, stand in the shower because I'm breaking down the door.

NORMA   *(Getting in front of the door)* Roy, don't get crazy.

ROY   *(Preparing himself for a run at the door)* Get out of my way.

NORMA   Roy, she'll come out. Just talk nicely to her.

ROY   *(Waving her away)* We already had nice talking. Now we're gonna have door breaking. *(Through the door)* All right, Mimsey, I'm coming in!

NORMA   No, Roy, don't! Don't!

(She gets out of the way as ROY *hurls his body, led by his shoulder, with full force against the door. It doesn't budge. He stays against the door silently a second; he doesn't react. Then he says calmly and softly)*

ROY   Get a doctor.

NORMA   *(Standing below the door)* I knew it. I knew it.

ROY   *(Drawing back from the door)* Don't tell me I knew it, just get a doctor. *(Through the door)* I'm not coming in, Mimsey, because my arm is broken.

NORMA   Let me see it. Can you move your fingers?

(Moves to him and examines his fingers)

ROY   *(Through the door)* Are you happy now? Your mother has torn stockings and your father has a broken arm. How much longer is this gonna go on?

NORMA   *(Moving* ROY's *fingers)* It's not broken, you can move your fingers. Give me four dollars with your other hand, I have to get stockings.

(She starts to go into his pockets. He slaps her hands away)

ROY   Are you crazy moving a broken arm?

NORMA   Two dollars, I'll get a cheap pair.

ROY   *(As though she were a lunatic)* I'm not carrying any cash today. Rented, everything is rented.

NORMA   I can't rent stockings. Don't you even have a charge-plate?

(Starts to go through his pockets again)

ROY   *(Slaps her hands away. Then pointing dramatically)* Wait in the Green Room! You're no use to me here, go wait in the Green Room!

NORMA   With torn stockings?

ROY   Stand behind the rented potted plant. *(Takes her by the arm. . . .*

Confidentially) They're going to call from downstairs any second asking where the bride is. And *I'm* the one who's going to have to speak to them. *Me! Me! Me! (The phone rings. Pushing her toward the phone)* That's them. *You* speak to them!

NORMA   What happened to *me me me*?
    (The phone rings again)

ROY   *(Moving to the bathroom door)* Answer it. Answer it.
    (The phone rings again)

NORMA   *(Moving to the phone)* What am I going to say to them?

ROY   I don't know. Maybe something'll come to you as you're talking.

NORMA   *(Picks the phone up)* Hello? . . . Oh, Mr. Eisler . . . Yes, it certainly is the big moment.
    (She forces a merry laugh)

ROY   Stall 'em. Stall 'em. Just keep stalling him. Whatever you do, stall 'em!
    (Turns to the door)

NORMA   *(On the phone)* Yes, we'll be down in two minutes.
    (Hangs up)

ROY   *(Turns back to her)* Are you crazy? What did you say that for? I told you to stall him.

NORMA   I stalled him. You got two minutes. What do you want from me?

ROY   *(Shakes his arm at her)* You always panic. The minute there's a little crisis, you always go to pieces and panic.

NORMA   *(Shakes her arm back at him)* Don't wave your broken arm at me. Why don't you use it to get your daughter out of the bathroom?

ROY   *(Very angry, kneeling to her on the bed)* I could say something to you now.

NORMA   *(Confronting him, kneels in turn on the bed)* Then why don't you say it?

ROY   Because it would lead to a fight. And I don't want to spoil this day for you. *(He gets up and crosses back to the bathroom door)* Mimsey, this is your father speaking . . . I think you know I'm not a violent man. I can be stern and strict, but I have never once been violent. Except when I'm angry. And I am really angry now, Mimsey. You can ask your mother.

(Moves away so NORMA *can get to the door)*

NORMA *(Crossing to the bathroom door)* Mimsey, this is your mother speaking. It's true, darling, your father is very angry.

ROY *(Moving back to the door)* This is your father again, Mimsey. If you have a problem you want to discuss, unlock the door and we'll discuss it. I'm not going to ask you this again, Mimsey. I've reached the end of my patience. I'm gonna count to three . . . and by God, I'm warning you, young lady, by the time I've reached three . . . *this door better be open*!

(Moving away to below the bed) All right—One! . . . Two! . . . THREE! *(There is no reply or movement from behind the door.* ROY *helplessly sinks down on the foot of the bed)* . . . Where did we fail her?

NORMA *(Crosses to the far side of the bed, consoling him as she goes, and sits on the edge)* We didn't fail her.

ROY They're playing "Here Comes the Bride" downstairs and she's barricaded in a toilet—we must have failed her.

NORMA *(Sighs)* All right, if it makes you any happier, we failed her.

ROY You work and you dream and you hope and you save your whole life for this day, and in one click of a door, suddenly everything crumbles. Why? What's the answer?

NORMA It's not your fault, Roy. Stop blaming yourself.

ROY I'm not blaming myself. I know *I've* done my best.

NORMA *(Turns and looks at him)* What does that mean?

ROY It means we're not perfect. We make mistakes, we're only human. I've done my best and we failed her.

NORMA Meaning *I* didn't do my best?

ROY   (*Turning to her*) I didn't say that. I don't know what your best is. Only *you* know what your best is. Did you do your best?

NORMA   Yes, I did my best.

ROY   And I did my best.

NORMA   Then we *both* did our best.

ROY   So it's not our fault.

NORMA   That's what I said before.

        (*They turn away from each other. Then*)

ROY   (*Softly*) Unless one of us didn't do our best.

NORMA   (*Jumping up and moving away*) I don't want to discuss it anymore.

ROY   All right, then what are we going to do?

NORMA   I'm having a heart attack, *you* come up with something.

ROY   How? All right, I'll go down and tell them.

        (*Gets up and moves to the bedroom door*)

NORMA   (*Moving to the door in front of him*) Tell them? Tell them what?

        (*As they move into the living room, she stops him above the sofa*)

ROY   I don't know. Those people down there deserve some kind of an explanation. They got all dressed up, didn't they?

NORMA   What are you going to say? You're going to tell them that my daughter is not going to marry their son and that she's locked herself in the bathroom?

ROY   What do you want me to do, start off with two good jokes? They're going to find out *some* time, aren't they?

NORMA   (*With great determination*) I'll tell you what you're going to do. If she's not out of there in five minutes, we're going to go out the back door and move to Seattle, Washington! . . . You don't think I'll be able to show my face in this city again, do you? (ROY *ponders this for a moment, then reassures her with a pat on the arm. Slowly he turns and moves into the bedroom. Suddenly, he loses control and lets his anger get the best of him. He grabs up the chair from the dresser, and brandishing it above his head, he dashes for the bathroom door, not even detouring around the bed but rather crossing right over it.* NORMA *screams and chases after him)* ROY!

(At the bathroom door, ROY *manages to stop himself in time from smashing the chair against the door, trembling with frustration and anger. Finally, exhausted, he puts the chair down below the door and straddles it, sitting leaning on the back.* NORMA *sinks into the bedroom armchair)*

ROY   . . .Would you believe it, last night I cried. Oh, yes. I turned my head into the pillow and lay there in the dark crying, because today I was losing my little girl. Some stranger was coming and taking my little Mimsey away from me . . . so I turned my back to you—and cried . . . Wait'll you hear what goes on *tonight*!

NORMA   *(Lost in her own misery)* I should have invited your cousin Lillie. *(Gestures to the heavens)* She wished this on me, I know it. *(Suddenly* ROY *begins to chuckle.* NORMA *looks at him. He chuckles louder, although there is clearly no joy in his laughter)* Do you find something funny about this?

ROY   Yes, I find something funny about this. I find it funny that I hired a photographer for three hundred dollars. I find it hysterical that the wedding pictures are going to be you and me in front of a locked bathroom! *(Gets up and puts the chair aside)* All right, I'm through sitting around waiting for that door to open.

(He crosses to the bedroom window and tries to open it)

NORMA   *(Following after him)* What are you doing?

ROY   What do you think I'm doing?

(Finding it impossible to open it, he crosses to the living room and opens a window there. The curtains begin to blow in the breeze)

NORMA   *(Crosses after him)* If you're jumping, I'm going with you. You're not leaving *me* here alone.

ROY   *(Looking out the window)* I'm gonna crawl out along the ledge and get in through the bathroom window.

(He starts to climb out the window)

NORMA   Are you crazy? It's seven stories up. You'll kill yourself.

(She grabs hold of him)

ROY   It's four steps, that's all. It's no problem, I'm telling you. Now will you let go of me.

NORMA   *(Struggling to keep him from getting out the window)* Roy, no! Don't do this. We'll leave her in the bathroom. Let the hotel worry about her. Don't go out on the ledge.

(In desperation, she grabs hold of one of the tails of his coat)

ROY   *(Half out the window, trying to get out as she holds onto his coat)* You're gonna rip my coat. Let go or you're gonna rip my coat. *(As he tries to pull away from her, his coat rips completely up the back, right up to the collar. He stops and slowly comes back into the room. NORMA has frozen in misery by the bedroom door after letting go of the coat. ROY draws himself up with great dignity and control. He slowly turns and moves into the bedroom, stopping by the bed. With great patience, he calls toward the bathroom)* Hey, you in there . . . Are you happy now? Your mother's got torn stockings and your father's got a rented ripped coat. Some wedding it's gonna be. *(Exploding, he crosses back to the open window in the living room)* Get out of my way!

NORMA   *(Puts hand to her head)* I'm getting dizzy. I think I'm going to pass out.

ROY   *(Getting her out of the way)* . . . You can pass out after the wedding . . . *(He goes out the window and onto the ledge)* Call room service. I want a double Scotch the minute I get back. *(And he disappears from view as he moves across the ledge. NORMA runs into the bedroom and catches a glimpse of him as he passes the bedroom window, but then he disappears once more)*

NORMA   *(Bemoaning her fate)* . . . He'll kill himself. He'll fall and kill himself, that's the way my luck's been going all day. *(She staggers away from the window and leans on the bureau)* I'm not going to look. I'll just wait until I hear a scream. *(The telephone rings and* NORMA *screams in fright)* Aggghhh! . . . I thought it was him . . . *(She crosses to the phone by the bed. The telephone rings again)* Oh, God, what am I going to say? *(She picks it up)* Hello? . . . Oh, Mr. Eisler. Yes, we're coming . . . My husband's getting Mimsey now . . . We'll be right down. Have some more hors d'oeuvres . . . Oh, thank you. It certainly *is* the happiest day of my life. *(She hangs up)* No, I'm going to tell him I've got a husband dangling over Fifty-ninth Street. *(As she crosses back to the opened window, a sudden torrent of rain begins to fall. As she gets to the window and sees it)* I knew it! I knew it! It had to happen . . . *(She gets closer to the window and tries to look out)* Are you all right, Roy? . . . Roy? *(There's no answer)* He's not all right, he fell. *(She staggers into the bedroom)* He fell, he fell, he fell, he fell . . . He's dead, I know it. *(She collapses onto the armchair)* He's laying there in a puddle in front of Trader Vic's . . . I'm passing out. This time I'm really passing out! *(And she passes out on the chair, legs and arms spread-eagled. The doorbell rings; she jumps right up)* I'm coming! I'm coming! Help me, whoever you are, help me! *(She rushes through the bedroom into the living room and to the front door)* Oh, please, somebody, help me, please!

    (She opens the front door and ROY *stands there dripping wet, fuming, exhausted and with clothes disheveled and his hair mussed)*

ROY   *(Staggering into the room and weakly leaning on the mantelpiece. It takes a moment for him to catch his breath.* NORMA, *concerned, follows him)* She locked the window too. I had to climb in through a strange bedroom. There may be a lawsuit.

Lives of the Saints

(an abridged excerpt from the novel)

Nancy Lemann

Receptions can also be tumultuous, as observed by one guest at a humid New Orleans affair replete with the bride's old flames, wastrel youth and a besotted father standing on his front lawn, bellowing, "My daughter is a delicate magnolia blossom!"

Brows were being mopped with white handkerchiefs, among white summer suits and seersucker suits, against a profusion of green in the Stewarts' garden. Everything was green and sumptuous and still, with green-and-white striped tents set up and the principals wearing white ties and tails. There were deck chairs set up in the garden, with people reeling around among them. It was stiflingly hot. Elderly gentlemen in advanced stages of disrepair were sitting in a row of deck chairs at the far side of the garden, all in their white summer suits.

The wedding was at three, and the reception started shortly after, but showed no signs of abating, though it was almost ten.

Henry Laines was screaming my name at the top of his lungs on the dance floor, not unlike the way he used to scream for Mary Grace, his bride, in the garden of his house at night. No one thought it was unusual that Henry Laines should be screaming my name instead of hers at his wedding reception on the dance floor, because everyone was too drunk to care. That is what it is like at parties where everyone is too drunk.

It was like slow motion when Henry Laines began to scream my name; a certain hush came over the dance floor, and a few people, particularly Claude Collier, gave Henry Laines a funny, somewhat pitying look from across the room. I noticed that. Claude Collier stood with his hands in his pockets, calmly contemplating the scene. His brow was furrowed, and he was squinting slightly. He was chewing a straw. . . .

"I think Henry is falling apart," Claude Collier said to me.

Henry Laines had already had two breakdowns since the ceremony.

"It's been a long day. He's tired. He's falling apart," said Claude mildly in a calm tone, slightly deadpan. Then Claude Collier looked at me intently. Claude Collier made the world seem kind. . . .

I surveyed the crowd, looking for people I knew. Mr. Walter Stewart, father of the bride, was an extremely large and loud man. He could be heard above the crowd. His blond wife was a person of whom he appeared to be only remotely fond, or even aware. She could spend an entire afternoon talking about what hat she wore when she was fifteen. She could also tell you who married who in the entire city and what scandals they caused. But her frivolity was heroic. She did it on purpose. Her husband ignored her, and she had lost her favorite son in a car wreck. She was an intelligent woman, but she just talked about what hat she wore when she was fifteen. Only the truly gallant, so it is said, are light-hearted in adversity.

Mrs. Walter Stewart did her duty in the world, without inquiring why, as though spurred on by the largeness of her husband and three remaining sons. Mr. Stewart had just recovered from his third heart attack. He was so large and robust it appeared he might endure a whole succession of heart attacks. He also had five hysterical, vivacious daughters, their husbands, their screaming children, and their black maids, all of whom were strewn in a panorama throughout the house.

His aging mother had come to live with them after his first heart attack. She was a woman with a grand and remote past. But quite like her daughter-in-law—because there was no subject dearer to Mr. Stewart's mother's heart than the subject of what hat she wore when she was fifteen. They both spent many hours talking about details of girlhood attire, and other lamebrained elements of clothing through the decades.

Mr. Walter Stewart came up and put his arms around me. I couldn't reach his cheek to kiss, but tried awkwardly, and succeeded in pressing my glasses lens into his cheek.

But he took my hand and said, "You are very dear to me, young lady."

Large, beefy, and handsome, with watery blue eyes, he invited me back into his house—or rather, ordered me in. Then he took me into his duck-hunting room and showed me his rifles. I politely admired his rifles, and he launched into a soliloquy about hunting and the thrill of the chase. Then he went off to stand on the front lawn of his mansion, where he called out to passersby—"My daughter is a delicate magnolia blossom!" or "I love my baby doll!"—in his gravel-voiced baritone. "She's my favorite, you know!" he advised the public. "She was always my favorite."

The best part of the night was when Claude Collier came up and turned my collar down and called me Darling.

I have found there is something about a turned-up collar that makes people want to turn it back down. It grips them with an overpowering desire to come over to you and—with a glazed, fond look in their eyes—turn your collar down.

But when Claude was turning my collar down, he held it so shockingly tenderly that I had to look away, as though you are so far from those you love that you drift out of time. I couldn't even look at him because it was like that. It was also shocking because it was uncharacteristic. I had known him for so many years.

"Everyone is falling apart," he said. He spoke in his calm deadpan. "But you're so pretty that it's taking advantage of some of that which would have been wasted," he added incoherently.

In the time that it took me to drink one gin and tonic, he would drink three. Alcohol was no stranger to him.

"No, no," I said, "Don't say a thing like that."

Then he called me Darling.

He was wearing a yellow tie, a wrinkled dark blue suit, and an overstarched white shirt. His tie was strewn over his shoulder and around the back as though it were strangling him. He was absentminded, disheveled, not vain. Vanity is worse than any vice, in my opinion. He had none. It was this which made him handsome. . . .

Claude walked up and started overwhelming Mrs. Stewart with his politeness. He was always polite. It was one of his greatest traits. It is hard to be truly polite. It is an elegant trait.

I felt like I was going into a stupor. I could hear Mr. Stewart quoting from a famous book he owned that he always quoted from, which was a history of the battles of the Civil War written entirely in verse. It filled me with dread.

"Let me tell you something about women," I could hear Mr. Stewart saying. "You have to treat women gently because they're weak. Young girls should be sheltered. They shouldn't be allowed to have affairs. One affair, and they're ruined. I pity women. After one affair, they're ruined. Who would want them?"

Oh, God, I thought. He was a law professor and had a tendency to lecture on all occasions. He often aired his private views for the benefit of large groups. He took a particular relish in quotation. I could hear him quoting from the Bible: " 'Woman, thou shouldst ever go in the sackcloth and mourning, thy eyes filled with tears. Thou hast brought about the ruin of mankind.' "

He was looking remorsefully into the eyes of some poor unsuspecting woman standing next to him, to gain a histrionic effect. As though off in a reverie, he turned dazed eyes on his youngest son.

"Peter, I'll tell you what Jeb Stuart used to say." Mr. Stewart looked raptly off into space. " 'All I ask of fate is that I may be killed leading a cavalry charge.' " . . .

I went back to Claude and Mrs. Stewart the elder, who were sitting there drinking like a couple of fish and chain-smoking. Every so often Mrs. Stewart lapsed into a coughing fit brought on by her dissipations.

Claude leaned over to me and said in a low tone, "I'm so drunk."

He had a little habit of calmly and obliviously shredding napkins, match-books, and cigarette packages, and he had filled about three ashtrays with shreddings. You could always tell a room in which Claude had recently visited, because its table tops would be strewn with shreddings and chewed pencils and chewed straws and other wreckage.

"Stop shredding things," I said.

He took a pencil out of his pocket and started eating the eraser. Then he leaned over to me and confided, "I'm so drunk."

"I seem to remember hearing this conversation somewhere before," I said.

He picked up a napkin.

"Mrs. Stewart? Louise? Can I get you a drink?" Claude said loudly.

"No, thank you," I said significantly.

"Why, I'd love a drink, Claude," said Mrs. Stewart gaily.

He walked over to the bar and got the drinks. He joked around with the bar-tender, apparently having a strong bond of affection with him. Then Claude went over to the bandstand and told some kind of joke to the orchestra, who all appeared to be in stitches from it, having found it so unbearably hilarious, whatever it was, that they stopped playing and were all drooping over their seats in hilarity.

A group of debauchees were sitting in a corner by the bar with napkins tied on their heads and loaves of French bread stuck in their breast pockets, even though they were grown, twenty-eight-year-old men. "CC!" they screamed when Claude drew near, and everyone seemed to get very maudlin, with Claude bending down to shake hands, as though he hadn't seen them in a Very Long Time, as opposed to one minute ago.

The men were calling each other *sweetheart* and *baby*. Things seemed to be getting more maudlin. Claude walked up and down the hall among the revelers strewn in chairs along the walls, stooping down to shake hands with elderly men. Then Claude did jokes for his cronies, which put the entire party in even more of a slapstick mood than even the napkin-heads had been in. Devil-may-care, that was their attitude, after Claude got through with them.

But I saw him take a pack of cigarettes out, and his hands were shaking so badly when he tried to light the match that I saw him give it up and leave off trying. He put the package surreptitiously back in his pocket. . . .

Mr. Sully Legendre was weaving toward us. He had silver hair parted in the middle, making melodramatic wings on either side of his face, and a glamorous silver mustache. The society column in the newspaper referred to him as "the hyper-handsome Sully Legendre."

This hopeless burden fell on his wife. That girl got her heart broke.

He gazed at us with his heavy-lidded eyes, and then screamed in a maniacal voice, "BABY!"

Then he clasped me to his bosom.

"CLAUDE, DAWLIN!" he screamed to my companion.

Heads turned. Silence fell upon suddenly hushed conversations. It was as though Mr. Sully Legendre were returned, at last, from the Odyssey.

"BABY!" he screamed again in histrionic amazement and joy. "IT'S LOUISE BROWN!" he screamed, and stood riveted in amazement.

The man was plainly falling apart.

Claude made normal remarks and pretended that everything was normal—and Mr. Legendre subsided somewhat, though he still displayed the mock-amazed congeniality of New Orleanians confronted with the spectacle of one another.

Mary Grace ran into the house in tears. Someone told us that Mr. Legendre had just crashed into the brick wall in the garden while attempting to drive his car. Claude said we should make him lie down. It was always like this in the Stewarts' house. Their household depended on emotional crisis to exist.

"Claude, dawlin, I heard you were moving to New Yawk," said Mr. Legendre while we led him upstairs. "Don't go, baby—New Yawk's not the kind of place for you." Mr. Legendre gazed at Claude with his sentimental eyes.

"That must have been a rumor," said Claude. "I'm not going anywhere."

I hate rumors.

"Don't go, dawlin," said Mr. Legendre. "Come and have a drink with me next week and I'll tell you why you shouldn't go. Louise, dawlin, come and have a drink with me next week and I'll tell you why Claude shouldn't go. We can go to the park and just sit under a tree."

I would love to go and have a drink with Mr. Legendre and sit under a tree.

We got him into one of the rooms upstairs and made him lie down. There was a packed suitcase by the bed which was filled with summer whites. Apparently mistaking it, in his stupor, for Claude's suitcase for his departure to New York, Mr. Legendre gazed at it from the bed.

"Starched white pants from Louisiana," he said sadly. "They won't understand that up there in New Yawk."

Then he passed out—not realizing, perhaps, the Profound Truth of his remark.

"Everyone is falling apart," said Claude. . . .

They say April is the cruelest month—and maybe it is so. But it is not so in the tropics. It is not like the North, where spring comes like an idiot whose wake is strewn with garish flowers. The New Orleans spring is more subtle, and gentle to bear. Everything remains the same throughout the year, overgrown and green.

. . . I saw Mary Grace in her traveling clothes, standing under the oaks in the garden, appearing to be having some sort of breakdown. Claude was standing there with her, with that stricken look on his face that he got when people were having breakdowns. I heard her say things only a drunk girl would say. Only a girl who was very drunk would say them. It was one of those swift and irrevocable moments during which someone's whole life is ruined. But Claude stood there stalwart and tall, with something understated in his eyes.

He took her face in his hand and said something, which I could not hear, but I do not doubt that he gave her kind advice, and that he wished her well.

Henry Laines was also falling apart. He was made that way. He was made to scream wild declarations of love to women in dressing rooms and gardens, and then throw pots and pans on them. And then he was made to get in rages and have jazz music and crashes coming out of his apartment across the garden and have nothing in his icebox except an old head of broccoli.

Life ran high in Mary Grace, and I admired her for that—it takes generosity to love, no matter what the circumstance, and she had loved many. But she was in a state of Total Chaos, among the madcap palms and honorable oaks, as society shed its bloodshot eyes upon the scene.

Everyone was leaving. The wastrel-youth contingent was making plans to meet later at the Lafayette Hotel for binges.

I was walking down the Garden District street, watching everyone "tank up," as my companion put it, in their cars, in alleys, and walking down the street, everyone with their plastic cups and glasses washing liquor down their throats. People were sitting in parked cars about to take off, but pouring liquor down their throats, first.

Tom, the bride's old flame, was strewn upon the ground, tangled up in the wires of his Walkman, passed out underneath his car.

So when the wastrel-youth contingent had departed, the old sat at tables in the house, with some of the men in tuxedos, against the ancient walls, with brandy glasses and cigars, a more than pretty sight, and looked back to view with fond dismay the crises of their own youth.

The Bridal Party

F. Scott Fitzgerald

Weddings are not only a transition for the bride and groom but, in the case of this Fitzgerald gem first published in 1930, for the bride's ex-lover and for the Lost Generation itself.

There was the usual insincere little note saying: "I wanted you to be the first to know." It was a double shock to Michael, announcing, as it did, both the engagement and the imminent marriage; which, moreover, was to be held, not in New York, decently and far away, but here in Paris under his very nose, if that could be said to extend over the Protestant Episcopal Church of the Holy Trinity, Avenue George-Cinq. The date was two weeks off, early in June.

At first Michael was afraid and his stomach felt hollow. When he left the hotel that morning, the *femme de chambre*, who was in love with his fine, sharp profile and his pleasant buoyancy, scented the hard abstraction that had settled over him. He walked in a daze to his bank, he bought a detective story at Smith's on the Rue de Rivoli, he sympathetically stared for a while at a faded panorama of the battlefields in a tourist-office window and cursed a Greek tout who followed him with a half-displayed packet of innocuous postcards warranted to be very dirty indeed.

But the fear stayed with him, and after a while he recognized it as the fear that now he would never be happy. He had met Caroline Dandy when she was seventeen, possessed her young heart all through her first season in New York, and then lost her, slowly, tragically, uselessly, because he had no money and could make no money; because, with all the energy and good will in the world, he could not find himself; because, loving him still, Caroline had lost faith and begun to see him as something pathetic, futile and shabby, outside the great, shining stream of life toward which she was inevitably drawn.

Since his only support was that she loved him, he leaned weakly on that;

the support broke, but still he held on to it and was carried out to sea and washed up on the French coast with its broken pieces still in his hands. He carried them around with him in the form of photographs and packets of correspondence and a liking for a maudlin popular song called "Among My Souvenirs." He kept clear of other girls, as if Caroline would somehow know it and reciprocate with a faithful heart. Her note informed him that he had lost her forever.

It was a fine morning. In front of the shops in the Rue de Castiglione, proprietors and patrons were on the sidewalk gazing upward, for the Graf Zeppelin, shining and glorious, symbol of escape and destruction—of escape, if necessary, through destruction—glided in the Paris sky. He heard a woman say in French that it would not astonish her if that commenced to let fall the bombs. Then he heard another voice, full of husky laughter, and the void in his stomach froze. Jerking about, he was face to face with Caroline Dandy and her fiancé.

"Why, Michael! Why, we were wondering where you were. I asked at the Guaranty Trust, and the Morgan and Company, and finally sent a note to the National City—"

Why didn't they back away? Why didn't they back right up, walking backward down the Rue de Castiglione, across the Rue de Rivoli, through the Tuileries Gardens, still walking backward as fast as they could till they grew vague and faded out across the river?

"This is Hamilton Rutherford, my fiancé."

"We've met before."

"At Pat's, wasn't it?"

"And last spring in the Ritz Bar."

"Michael, where have you been keeping yourself?"

"Around here." This agony. Previews of Hamilton Rutherford flashed before his eyes—a quick series of pictures, sentences. He remembered hearing that he had bought a seat in 1920 for a hundred and twenty-five thousand of borrowed money, and just before the break sold it for more than half a million. Not handsome like Michael, but vitally attractive, confident, authoritative, just the right height over Caroline there—Michael had always been too short for Caroline when they danced.

Rutherford was saying: "No, I'd like it very much if you'd come to the bachelor dinner. I'm taking the Ritz Bar from nine o'clock on. Then right after the wedding there'll be a reception and breakfast at the Hotel George-Cinq."

"And, Michael, George Packman is giving a party day after tomorrow at Chez Victor, and I want you to be sure and come. And also to tea Friday at Jebby West's; she'd want to have you if she knew where you were. What's your hotel, so we can send you an invitation? You see, the reason we decided to have it over here is because mother has been sick in a nursing home here and the whole clan is in Paris. Then Hamilton's mother's being here too—"

The entire clan; they had always hated him, except her mother; always discouraged his courtship. What a little counter he was in this game of families and money! Under his hat his brow sweated with the humiliation of the fact that for all his misery he was worth just exactly so many invitations. Frantically he began to mumble something about going away.

Then it happened—Caroline saw deep into him, and Michael knew that she saw. She saw through to his profound woundedness, and something quivered inside her, died out along the curve of her mouth and in her eyes. He had moved her. All the unforgettable impulses of first love had surged up once more; their hearts had in some way touched across two feet of Paris sunlight. She took her fiancé's arm suddenly, as if to steady herself with the feel of it.

They parted. Michael walked quickly for a minute; then he stopped, pretending to look in a window, and saw them farther up the street, walking fast into the Place Vendôme, people with much to do.

He had things to do also—he had to get his laundry.

"Nothing will ever be the same again," he said to himself. "She will never be happy in her marriage and I will never be happy at all anymore."

The two vivid years of his love for Caroline moved back around him like years in Einstein's physics. Intolerable memories arose—of rides in the Long Island moonlight; of a happy time at Lake Placid with her cheeks so cold there, but warm just underneath the surface; of a despairing afternoon in a little café on Forty-eighth Street in the last sad months when their marriage had come to seem impossible.

"Come in," he said aloud.

The concierge with a telegram; brusque because Mr. Curly's clothes were a little shabby. Mr. Curly gave few tips; Mr. Curly was obviously a *petit client*.

Michael read the telegram.

"An answer?" the concierge asked.

"No," said Michael, and then, on an impulse: "Look."

"Too bad—too bad," said the concierge. "Your grandfather is dead."

"Not too bad," said Michael. "It means that I come into a quarter of a million dollars."

Too late by a single month; after the first flush of the news his misery was deeper than ever. Lying awake in bed that night, he listened endlessly to the caravan of a circus moving through the street from one Paris fair to another.

When the last van had rumbled out of hearing and the corners of the furniture were pastel blue with the dawn, he was still thinking of the look in Caroline's eyes that morning—the look that seemed to say: "Oh, why couldn't you have done something about it? Why couldn't you have been stronger, made me marry you? Don't you see how sad I am?"

Michael's fists clenched.

"Well, I won't give up till the last moment," he whispered. "I've had all the

F. SCOTT FITZGERALD   35

bad luck so far, and maybe it's turned at last. One takes what one can get, up to the limit of one's strength, and if I can't have her, at least she'll go into this marriage with some of me in her heart."

II.

Accordingly he went to the party at Chez Victor two days later, upstairs and into the little salon off the bar where the party was to assemble for cocktails. He was early; the only other occupant was a tall lean man of fifty. They spoke.

"You waiting for George Packman's party?"

"Yes. My name's Michael Curly."

"My name's—"

Michael failed to catch the name. They ordered a drink, and Michael supposed that the bride and groom were having a gay time.

"Too much so," the other agreed, frowning. "I don't see how they stand it. We all crossed on the boat together; five days of that crazy life and then two weeks of Paris. You"—he hesitated, smiling faintly—"you'll excuse me for saying that your generation drinks too much."

"Not Caroline."

"No, not Caroline. She seems to take only a cocktail and a glass of champagne, and then she's had enough, thank God. But Hamilton drinks too much and all this crowd of young people drink too much. Do you live in Paris?"

"For the moment," said Michael.

"I don't like Paris. My wife—that is to say, my ex-wife, Hamilton's mother— lives in Paris."

"You're Hamilton Rutherford's father?"

"I have that honor. And I'm not denying that I'm proud of what he's done; it was just a general comment."

"Of course."

Michael glanced up nervously as four people came in. He felt suddenly that his dinner coat was old and shiny; he had ordered a new one that morning. The people who had come in were rich and at home in their richness with one another—a dark, lovely girl with a hysterical little laugh whom he had met before; two confident men whose jokes referred invariably to last night's scandal and tonight's potentialities, as if they had important roles in a play that extended indefinitely into the past and the future. When Caroline arrived, Michael had scarcely a moment of her, but it was enough to note that, like all the others, she was strained and tired. She was pale beneath her rouge; there were shadows under her eyes. With a mixture of relief and wounded vanity, he found himself placed far from her and at another table; he needed a moment to adjust himself to his surroundings. This was not like the immature set in which he and Caroline had moved; the men were more than thirty and had an air of sharing the best of this world's good. Next to him was Jebby West, whom he knew; and, on the other side, a jovial man who immediately began to talk to Michael about a stunt for the bachelor dinner: They were going to hire a French girl to appear with an actual baby in her arms, crying: "Hamilton, you can't desert me now!" The idea seemed stale and unamusing to Michael, but its originator shook with anticipatory laughter.

Farther up the table there was talk of the market—another drop today, the most appreciable since the crash; people were kidding Rutherford about it: "Too bad, old man. You better not get married, after all."

Michael asked the man on his left, "Has he lost a lot?"

"Nobody knows. He's heavily involved, but he's one of the smartest young men in Wall Street. Anyhow, nobody ever tells you the truth."

It was a champagne dinner from the start, and toward the end it reached a pleasant level of conviviality, but Michael saw that all these people were too weary to be exhilarated by any ordinary stimulant; for weeks they had drunk cocktails before meals like Americans, wines and brandies like Frenchmen, beer like Germans, whiskey-and-soda like the English, and as they were no longer in the twenties, this preposterous *mélange*, that was like some gigantic cocktail in a nightmare, served only to make them temporarily less conscious of the mistakes of the night before. Which is to say that it was not really a gay party; what gayety existed was displayed in the few who drank nothing at all.

But Michael was not tired, and the champagne stimulated him and made his misery less acute. He had been away from New York for more than eight months and most of the dance music was unfamiliar to him, but at the first bars of the "Painted Doll," to which he and Caroline had moved through so much happiness and despair the previous summer, he crossed to Caroline's table and asked her to dance.

She was lovely in a dress of thin ethereal blue, and the proximity of her crackly yellow hair, of her cool and tender gray eyes, turned his body clumsy and rigid; he stumbled with their first step on the floor. For a moment it seemed that there was nothing to say; he wanted to tell her about his inheritance, but the idea seemed abrupt, unprepared for.

"Michael, it's so nice to be dancing with you again."

He smiled grimly.

"I'm so happy you came," she continued. "I was afraid maybe you'd be silly and stay away. Now we can be just good friends and natural together. Michael, I want you and Hamilton to like each other."

The engagement was making her stupid; he had never heard her make such a series of obvious remarks before.

"I could kill him without a qualm," he said pleasantly, "but he looks like a good man. He's fine. What I want to know is, what happens to people like me who aren't able to forget?"

As he said this he could not prevent his mouth from dropping suddenly, and glancing up, Caroline saw, and her heart quivered violently, as it had the other morning.

"Do you mind so much, Michael?"

"Yes."

For a second as he said this, in a voice that seemed to have come up from his shoes, they were not dancing; they were simply clinging together. Then she leaned away from him and twisted her mouth into a lovely smile.

"I didn't know what to do at first, Michael. I told Hamilton about you—that I'd cared for you an awful lot—but it didn't worry him, and he was right. Because I'm over you now—yes, I am. And you'll wake up some sunny morning and be over me just like that."

He shook his head stubbornly.

"Oh, yes. We weren't for each other. I'm pretty flighty, and I need somebody like Hamilton to decide things. It was that more than the question of—of—"

"Of money." Again he was on the point of telling her what had happened, but again something told him it was not the time.

"Then how do you account for what happened when we met the other day," he demanded helplessly—"what happened just now? When we just pour toward each other like we used to—as if we were one person, as if the same blood was flowing through both of us?"

"Oh, don't," she begged him. "You mustn't talk like that; everything's decided now. I love Hamilton with all my heart. It's just that I remember certain things in the past and I feel sorry for you—for us— for the way we were."

Over her shoulder, Michael saw a man come toward them to cut in. In a panic he danced her away, but inevitably the man came on.

"I've got to see you alone, if only for a minute," Michael said quickly. "When can I?"

"I'll be at Jebby West's tea tomorrow," she whispered as a hand fell politely upon Michael's shoulder.

But he did not talk to her at Jebby West's tea. Rutherford stood next to her, and each brought the other into all conversations. They left early. The next morning the wedding cards arrived in the first mail.

Then Michael, grown desperate with pacing up and down his room, determined on a bold stroke; he wrote to Hamilton Rutherford, asking him for a rendezvous the following afternoon. In a short telephone communication Rutherford agreed, but for a day later than Michael had asked. And the wedding was only six days away.

They were to meet in the bar of the Hotel Jena. Michael knew what he would say: "See here, Rutherford, do you realize the responsibility you're taking in going through with this marriage? Do you realize the harvest of trouble and regret you're sowing in persuading a girl into something contrary to the instincts of her heart?" He would explain that the barrier between Caroline and himself had been an artificial one and was now removed, and demand that the matter be put up to Caroline frankly before it was too late.

Rutherford would be angry, conceivably there would be a scene, but Michael felt that he was fighting for his life now.

He found Rutherford in conversation with an older man, whom Michael had met at several of the wedding parties.

"I saw what happened to most of my friends," Rutherford was saying, "and I decided it wasn't going to happen to me. It isn't so difficult; if you take a girl with common sense, and tell her what's what, and do your stuff damn well, and play decently square with her, it's a marriage. If you stand for any nonsense at the beginning, it's one of these arrangements—within five years the man gets out, or else the girl gobbles him up and you have the usual mess."

"Right!" agreed his companion enthusiastically. "Hamilton, boy, you're right."

Michael's blood boiled slowly.

"Doesn't it strike you," he inquired coldly, "that your attitude went out of fashion a hundred years ago?"

"No, it didn't," said Rutherford pleasantly, but impatiently. "I'm as modern as anybody. I'd get married in an aeroplane next Saturday if it'd please my girl."

"I don't mean that way of being modern. You can't take a sensitive woman —"

"Sensitive? Women aren't so darn sensitive. It's fellows like you who are sensitive; it's fellows like you they exploit — all your devotion and kindness and all that. They read a couple of books and see a few pictures because they haven't got anything else to do, and then they say they're finer in grain than you are, and to prove it they take the bit in their teeth and tear off for a fare-you-well — just about as sensitive as a fire horse."

"Caroline happens to be sensitive," said Michael in a clipped voice.

At this point the other man got up to go; when the dispute about the check had been settled and they were alone, Rutherford leaned back to Michael as if a question had been asked him.

"Caroline's more than sensitive," he said. "She's got sense."

His combative eyes, meeting Michael's, flickered with a gray light. "This all sounds pretty crude to you, Mr. Curly, but it seems to me that the average man nowadays just asks to be made a monkey of by some woman who doesn't even get any fun out of reducing him to that level. There are darn few men who possess their wives anymore, but I am going to be one of them."

To Michael it seemed time to bring the talk back to the actual situation: "Do you realize the responsibility you're taking?"

"I certainly do," interrupted Rutherford. "I'm not afraid of responsibility. I'll make the decisions — fairly, I hope, but anyhow they'll be final."

"What if you didn't start right?" said Michael impetuously. "What if your marriage isn't founded on mutual love?"

"I think I see what you mean," Rutherford said, still pleasant. "And since

you've brought it up, let me say that if you and Caroline had married, it wouldn't have lasted three years. Do you know what your affair was founded on? On sorrow. You got sorry for each other. Sorrow's a lot of fun for most women and for some men, but it seems to me that a marriage ought to be based on hope." He looked at his watch and stood up.

"I've got to meet Caroline. Remember, you're coming to the bachelor dinner day after tomorrow."

Michael felt the moment slipping away. "Then Caroline's personal feelings don't count with you?" he demanded fiercely.

"Caroline's tired and upset. But she has what she wants, and that's the main thing."

"Are you referring to yourself?" demanded Michael incredulously.

"Yes."

"May I ask how long she's wanted you?"

"About two years." Before Michael could answer, he was gone.

During the next two days Michael floated in an abyss of helplessness. The idea haunted him that he had left something undone that would sever this knot drawn tighter under his eyes. He phoned Caroline, but she insisted that it was physically impossible for her to see him until the day before the wedding, for which day she granted him a tentative rendezvous. Then he went to the bachelor dinner, partly in fear of an evening alone at his hotel, partly from a feeling that by his presence at that function he was somehow nearer to Caroline, keeping her in sight.

The Ritz Bar had been prepared for the occasion by French and American banners and by a great canvas covering one wall, against which the guests were invited to concentrate their proclivities in breaking glasses.

At the first cocktail, taken at the bar, there were many slight spillings from many trembling hands, but later, with the champagne, there was a rising tide of laughter and occasional bursts of song.

Michael was surprised to find what a difference his new dinner coat, his new silk hat, his new, proud linen made in his estimate of himself; he felt less resentment toward all these people for being so rich and assured. For the first time since he had left college he felt rich and assured himself; he felt that he was part of all this, and even entered into the scheme of Johnson, the practical joker, for the appearance of the woman betrayed, now waiting tranquilly in the room across the hall.

"We don't want to go too heavy," Johnson said, "because I imagine Ham's had a pretty anxious day already. Did you see Fullman Oil's sixteen points off this morning?"

"Will that matter to him?" Michael asked, trying to keep the interest out of his voice.

"Naturally. He's in heavily; he's always in everything heavily. So far he's had luck; anyhow, up to a month ago."

The glasses were filled and emptied faster now, and men were shouting at one another across the narrow table. Against the bar a group of ushers was being photographed, and the flash light surged through the room in a stifling cloud.

"Now's the time," Johnson said. "You're to stand by the door, remember, and we're both to try and keep her from coming in—just till we get everybody's attention."

He went on out into the corridor, and Michael waited obediently by the door. Several minutes passed. Then Johnson reappeared with a curious expression on his face.

"There's something funny about this."

"Isn't the girl there?"

"She's there all right, but there's another woman there, too; and it's nobody we engaged either. She wants to see Hamilton Rutherford, and she looks as if she had something on her mind."

They went out into the hall. Planted firmly in a chair near the door sat an American girl a little worse for liquor, but with a determined expression on her face. She looked up at them with a jerk of her head.

"Well, j'tell him?" she demanded. "The name is Marjorie Collins, and he'll know it. I've come a long way, and I want to see him now and quick, or there's going to be more trouble than you ever saw." She rose unsteadily to her feet.

"You go in and tell Ham," whispered Johnson to Michael. "Maybe he'd better get out. I'll keep her here."

Back at the table, Michael leaned close to Rutherford's ear and, with a certain grimness, whispered:

"A girl outside named Marjorie Collins says she wants to see you. She looks as if she wanted to make trouble."

Hamilton Rutherford blinked and his mouth fell ajar; then slowly the lips came together in a straight line and he said in a crisp voice:

"Please keep her there. And send the head barman to me right away."

Michael spoke to the barman, and then, without returning to the table, asked quietly for his coat and hat. Out in the hall again, he passed Johnson and the girl without speaking and went out into the Rue Cambon. Calling a cab, he gave the address of Caroline's hotel.

His place was beside her now. Not to bring bad news, but simply to be with her when her house of cards came falling around her head.

Rutherford had implied that he was soft—well, he was hard enough not to give up the girl he loved without taking advantage of every chance within the pale of honor. Should she turn away from Rutherford, she would find him there.

She was in; she was surprised when he called, but she was still dressed and would be down immediately. Presently she appeared in a dinner gown, holding two blue telegrams in her hand. They sat down in armchairs in the deserted lobby.

"But, Michael, is the dinner over?"

"I wanted to see you, so I came away."

"I'm glad." Her voice was friendly, but matter-of-fact. "Because I'd just phoned your hotel that I had fittings and rehearsals all day tomorrow. Now we can have our talk after all."

"You're tired," he guessed. "Perhaps I shouldn't have come."

"No. I was waiting for Hamilton. Telegrams that may be important. He said he might go on somewhere, and that may mean any hour, so I'm glad to have someone to talk to."

Michael winced at the impersonality in the last phrase.

"Don't you care when he gets home?"

"Naturally," she said, laughing, "but I haven't got much to say about it, have I?"

"Why not?"

"I couldn't start by telling him what he could and couldn't do."

"Why not?"

"He wouldn't stand for it."

"He seems to want merely a housekeeper," said Michael ironically.

"Tell me about your plans, Michael," she asked quickly.

"My plans? I can't see any future after the day after tomorrow. The only real plan I ever had was to love you."

Their eyes brushed past each other's, and the look he knew so well was staring out at him from hers. Words flowed quickly from his heart:

"Let me tell you just once more how well I've loved you, never wavering for a moment, never thinking of another girl. And now when I think of all the years ahead without you, without any hope, I don't want to live, Caroline darling. I used to dream about our home, our children, about holding you in my arms and touching your face and hands and hair that used to belong to me, and now I just can't wake up."

Caroline was crying softly. "Poor Michael—poor Michael." Her hand reached out and her fingers brushed the lapel of his dinner coat. "I was so sorry for you the other night. You looked so thin, and as if you needed a new suit and somebody to take care of you." She sniffled and looked more closely at his coat. "Why, you've got a new suit! And a new silk hat! Why, Michael, how swell!" She laughed, suddenly cheerful through her tears. "You must have come into money, Michael; I never saw you so well turned out."

For a moment, at her reaction, he hated his new clothes.

"I have come into money," he said. "My grandfather left me about a quarter of a million dollars."

"Why, Michael," she cried, "how perfectly swell! I can't tell you how glad I am. I've always thought you were the sort of person who ought to have money."

"Yes, just too late to make a difference."

The revolving door from the street groaned around and Hamilton Rutherford came into the lobby. His face was flushed, his eyes were restless and impatient.

"Hello, darling; hello, Mr. Curly." He bent and kissed Caroline. "I broke away for a minute to find out if I had any telegrams. I see you've got them there." Taking them from her, he remarked to Curly, "That was an odd business in the bar, wasn't it? Especially as I understand some of you had a joke fixed up in the same line." He opened one of the telegrams, closed it and turned to Caroline with the divided expression of a man carrying two things in his head at once.

"A girl I haven't seen for two years turned up," he said. "It seemed to be some clumsy form of blackmail, for I haven't and never have had any sort of obligation toward her whatever."

"What happened?"

"The head barman had a Sûreté Générale man there in ten minutes and it was settled in the hall. The French blackmail laws make ours look like a sweet wish, and I gather they threw a scare into her that she'll remember. But it seems wiser to tell you."

"Are you implying that I mentioned the matter?" said Michael stiffly.

"No," Rutherford said slowly. "No, you were just going to be on hand. And since you're here, I'll tell you some news that will interest you even more."

He handed Michael one telegram and opened the other.

"This is in code," Michael said.

"So is this. But I've got to know all the words pretty well this last week. The two of them together mean that I'm due to start life all over."

Michael saw Caroline's face grow a shade paler, but she sat quiet as a mouse.

"It was a mistake and I stuck to it too long," continued Rutherford. "So you see I don't have all the luck, Mr. Curly. By the way, they tell me you've come into money."

"Yes," said Michael.

"There we are, then." Rutherford turned to Caroline. "You understand, darling, that I'm not joking or exaggerating. I've lost almost every cent I had and I'm starting life over."

Two pairs of eyes were regarding her—Rutherford's noncommittal and unrequiring, Michael's hungry, tragic, pleading. In a minute she had raised herself from the chair and with a little cry thrown herself into Hamilton Rutherford's arms.

"Oh, darling," she cried, "what does it matter! It's better; I like it better, honestly I do! I want to start that way; I want to! Oh, please don't worry or be sad even for a minute."

"All right, baby," said Rutherford. His hands stroked her hair gently for a moment; then he took his arm from around her.

"I promised to join the party for an hour," he said. "So I'll say good night, and I want you to go to bed soon and get a good sleep. Good night, Mr. Curly. I'm sorry to have let you in for all these financial matters."

But Michael had already picked up his hat and cane. "I'll go along with you," he said.

III.

It was such a fine morning. Michael's cutaway hadn't been delivered, so he felt rather uncomfortable passing before the cameras and moving-picture machines in front of the little church on the Avenue George-Cinq.

It was such a clean, new church that it seemed unforgivable not to be dressed properly, and Michael, white and shaky after a sleepless night, decided to stand in the rear. From there he looked at the back of Hamilton Rutherford, and the lacy, filmy back of Caroline, and the fat back of George Packman, which looked unsteady, as if it wanted to lean against the bride and groom.

The ceremony went on for a long time under gray flags and pennons overhead, under the thick beams of June sunlight slanting down through the tall windows upon the well-dressed people.

As the procession, headed by the bride and groom, started down the aisle, Michael realized with alarm he was just where everyone would dispense with their parade stiffness, become informal and speak to him.

So it turned out. Rutherford and Caroline spoke first to him; Rutherford grim with the strain of being married, and Caroline lovelier than he had ever seen her, floating all softly down through the friends and relatives of her youth, down through the past and forward to the future by the sunlit door.

Michael managed to murmur, "Beautiful, simply beautiful," and then other people passed and spoke to him—old Mrs. Dandy, straight from her sickbed and looking remarkably well, or carrying it off like the very fine old lady she was; and Rutherford's father and mother, ten years divorced, but walking side by side and looking made for each other and proud. Then all Caroline's sisters and their husbands and her little nephews in Eton suits, and then a long parade, all speaking to Michael because he was still standing paralyzed just at that point where the procession broke.

He wondered what would happen now. Cards had been issued for a reception at the George-Cinq; an expensive enough place, heaven knew. Would Rutherford try to go though with that on top of those disastrous telegrams? Evidently, for the procession outside was streaming up there through the June morning, three by three and four by four. On the corner the long dresses of girls, five abreast, fluttered many-colored in the wind. Girls had become gossamer again, perambulatory flora; such lovely fluttering dresses in the bright noon wind.

Michael needed a drink; he couldn't face that reception line without a drink. Diving into a side doorway of the hotel, he asked for the bar, whither a *chasseur* led him through half a kilometer of new American-looking passages.

But—how did it happen?—the bar was full. There were ten—fifteen men and two—four girls, all from the wedding, all needing a drink. There were cocktails and champagne in the bar; Rutherford's cocktails and champagne, as it turned out, for he had engaged the whole bar and the ballroom and the two great reception rooms and all the stairways leading up and down, and windows looking out over the whole square block of Paris. By and by Michael went and joined the long, slow drift of the receiving line. Through a flowery mist of "Such a lovely wedding," "My dear, you were simply lovely," "You're a lucky man, Rutherford" he passed down the line. When Michael came to Caroline, she took a single step forward and kissed him on the lips, but he felt no contact in the kiss; it was unreal and he floated on away from it. Old Mrs. Dandy, who had always liked him, held his hand for a minute and thanked him for the flowers he had sent when he heard she was ill.

"I'm so sorry not to have written; you know, we old ladies are grateful for—" The flowers, the fact that she had not written, the wedding—Michael saw that they all had the same relative importance to her now; she had married off five other children and seen two of the marriages go to pieces, and this scene, so poignant, so confusing to Michael, appeared to her simply a familiar charade in which she had played her part before.

A buffet luncheon with champagne was already being served at small tables and there was an orchestra playing in an empty ballroom. Michael sat down with Jebby West; he was still a little embarrassed at not wearing a morning coat, but he perceived now that he was not alone in the omission and felt better. "Wasn't Caroline divine?" Jebby West said. "So entirely self-possessed. I asked her this morning if she wasn't a little nervous at stepping off like this. And she said, 'Why should I be? I've been after him for two years, and now I'm just happy, that's all.'"

"It must be true," said Michael gloomily.

"What?"

"What you just said."

He had been stabbed, but, rather to his distress, he did not feel the wound.

He asked Jebby to dance. Out on the floor, Rutherford's father and mother were dancing together.

"It makes me a little sad, that," she said. "Those two hadn't met for years; both of them were married again and she divorced again. She went to the station to meet him when he came over for Caroline's wedding, and invited him to stay at her house in the Avenue du Bois with a whole lot of other people, perfectly proper, but he was afraid his wife would hear about it and not like it, so he went to a hotel. Don't you think that's sort of sad?"

An hour or so later Michael realized suddenly that it was afternoon. In one corner of the ballroom an arrangement of screens like a moving-picture stage had been set up and photographers were taking official pictures of the bridal party. The bridal party, still as death and pale as wax under the bright lights, appeared, to the dancers circling the modulated semidarkness of the ballroom, like those jovial or sinister groups that one comes upon in The Old Mill at an amusement park.

After the bridal party had been photographed, there was a group of the ushers; then the bridesmaids, the families, the children. Later, Caroline, active and excited, having long since abandoned the repose implicit in her flowing dress and great bouquet, came and plucked Michael off the floor.

"Now we'll have them take one of just old friends." Her voice implied that this was best, most intimate of all. "Come here, Jebby, George—not you, Hamilton; this is just my friends—Sally—"

A little after that, what remained of formality disappeared and the hours flowed easily down the profuse stream of champagne. In the modern fashion, Hamilton Rutherford sat at the table with his arm about an old girl of his and assured his guests, which included not a few bewildered but enthusiastic Europeans, that the party was not nearly at an end; it was to reassemble at Zelli's after midnight. Michael saw Mrs. Dandy, not quite over her illness, rise to go and become caught in polite group after group, and he spoke of it to one of her daughters, who thereupon forcibly abducted her mother and called her car. Michael felt very considerate and proud of himself after having done this, and drank much more champagne.

It's amazing," George Packman was telling him enthusiastically. "This show will cost Ham about five thousand dollars, and I understand they'll be just about his last. But did he countermand a bottle of champagne or a flower? Not he! He happens to have it—that young man. Do you know that T. G. Vance offered him a salary of fifty thousand dollars a year ten minutes before the wedding this morning? In another year he'll be back with the millionaires."

The conversation was interrupted by a plan to carry Rutherford out on communal shoulders—a plan which six of them put into effect, and then stood in the four-o'clock sunshine waving good-bye to the bride and groom. But there must have been a mistake somewhere, for five minutes later Michael saw both bride and groom descending the stairway to the reception, each with a glass of champagne held defiantly on high.

"This is our way of doing things," he thought. "Generous and fresh and free; a sort of Virginia-plantation hospitality, but at a different pace now, nervous as a ticker tape."

Standing unself-consciously in the middle of the room to see which was the American ambassador, he realized with a start that he hadn't thought of Caroline in hours. He looked about him with a sort of alarm, and then he saw her across the room, very bright and young, and radiantly happy. He saw Rutherford near her, looking at her as if he could never look long enough, and as Michael watched them they seemed to recede as he had wished them to do that day in the Rue de Castiglione—recede and fade off into joys and griefs of their own, into the years that would take the toll of Rutherford's fine pride and Caroline's young, moving beauty; fade far away, so that now he could scarcely see them, as if they were shrouded in something as misty as her white billowing dress.

Michael was cured. The ceremonial function, with its pomp and revelry, had stood for a sort of initiation into a life where even his regret could not follow them. All the bitterness melted out of him suddenly and the world reconstituted itself out of the youth and happiness that was all around him, profligate as the spring sunshine. He was trying to remember which one of the bridesmaids he had made a date to dine with tonight as he walked forward to bid Hamilton and Caroline Rutherford good-by.

The Wedding of the Century

(an excerpt)

Nicholas Davies

If nothing else, the wedding of Charles and Di is an object lesson in not getting caught up in the ritual's trappings at the expense of its emotional core—as well as the dangers of just going too big.

As July 29, the royal wedding day, approached, presents began to arrive from the people of Britain by every post—a total of three thousand before the end of June. Every morning Diana would go to the Wedding Present Center, especially set up in Buckingham Palace's private cinema, to view the latest arrivals. These were happy, exciting days for her, and she struck up a warm relationship with the palace staff.

The wedding was meticulously planned. There were endless meetings between Edward Adeane, Charles's private secretary, officials from the Lord Chamberlain's office, the Keeper of the Privy Purse, and the Master of the Household, who were working around the clock in preparation.

The Prince did not simply leave the arrangements to his staff. Few are aware of just how personally involved Charles was. The Lord Chamberlain traditionally organizes such rituals, but Charles demanded that he be informed of everything so that he could approve every detail. Charles even agreed to provide the commentary for a BBC television prewedding program.

Charles was determined to be married in St. Paul's Cathedral, even though Westminster Abbey was the traditional setting for royal weddings. He loved the beautiful old cathedral, and since it was considerably larger than Westminster, more guests could be accommodated.

The Lord Chamberlain, Lord Maclean, was distinctly uneasy about the choice of St. Paul's. It is much farther away from Buckingham Palace than Westminster, and the route is exposed, making security from a terrorist attack impossible to guarantee. He was mindful that in the past ten years, over two thousand people had been killed in the Irish troubles; the wedding might seem to the IRA an ideal opportunity for an assassination. The cost of policing the route would be prohibitive. Further, the Lord Chamberlain worried that not enough police and members of the armed forces would be available to line the route. But when he voiced his doubts, Charles replied simply, "Well, stand them further apart."

For security reasons, it was suggested that the Royal Family forgo the open carriages normally used on such occasions and use Rolls-Royces instead. The Queen would have none of it. At the time, nearly three million people were unemployed in Britain, the economy was in the doldrums, and not three weeks before there had been serious rioting in Liverpool, Manchester, and London. The IRA was active. A deranged man had fired blanks at the Queen during the Trooping of the Colors the previous month, and both the Pope and President Reagan had recently been attacked. But the Royal Family were united in their determination not to let the fear of assassination spoil the greatest day in the life of the Prince of Wales.

Prince Charles then set about planning the music, which was, he emphasized, his number-one priority. He had heard the opera singer Kiri Te Kanawa and, when he had met her on one of his official visits to New Zealand, had been enchanted by her attractive personality. He particularly hoped she would sing at his wedding because he wanted everything to be exactly right—which meant his favorite music should be played and sung by people he admired and liked. Te Kanawa was an excellent choice; her exquisite rendering of "Let the Bright Seraphim" was one of the most beautiful elements of the service.

Charles also selected the musical works for the choir and diligently studied the plan and all the timings for the ceremony. He was precise and fussy, knowing exactly and intuitively what would be best. This, after all, was what he had been trained for during much of his life: to produce royal spectacle. Diana probably had less say in the ceremony than the average bride, although her favorite hymn—"I Vow to Thee My Country"—was included.

Diana also had little say in the guest list. The Queen and the Royal Family made most of the decisions about whom to invite, but Diana and Earl Spencer were allowed to make suggestions.

The only real problem was whether to invite Diana's stepmother's mother, Barbara Cartland. The Royal Family, of course, are absolute sticklers for doing everything correctly and certainly did not want to appear vindictive or high-handed by not extending invitations that were proper and expected according to society's unwritten rules. The courtiers also recognized that Barbara Cartland had an extraordinary following of loyal readers whom the Palace would not wish to upset without good reason. On the other hand, the rules about a stepmother's mother are not as traditional or clear as rules about blood relatives. In the end, Charles allowed Diana to decide. Diana was adamant: no Barbara Cartland.

Earl Spencer noted one benefit to having the Royal Family take over all the arrangements. As he often joked, he did not pay a penny toward the cost of his daughter's wedding. . . .

The celebrations began in earnest the night before the wedding. A stupendous fireworks display burst over Hyde Park, and a chain of 101 beacons was lit on hills throughout England, Scotland, and Wales. Prince Charles set off the chain by lighting the first bonfire at 10:08 (it was scheduled for 10:00), and the displays began.

The whole of London seemed to be packed into the royal park. The massed bands of the Household Brigade of Guards played for two hours, together with the Morriston Orpheus Choir and the Choir of the Welsh Guards, and to round off the fantastic night, the Royal Horse Artillery fired salvos.

For hundreds of thousands of people who turned up in Hyde Park it was a night to remember. An estimated twelve thousand rockets were fired into the sky, and over two tons of explosives went off. The finale consisted of an exploding replica of Buckingham Palace, with huge sparkling likenesses of Charles and Diana filling the night sky. Nothing on such a grand scale had been seen since the spectacular pyrotechnics ordered by King George II, in 1749, to mark the Peace of Aix-la-Chapelle, and for which Handel wrote his *Music for the Royal Fireworks*.

Drinking, dancing, and partying carried on throughout the night. Such a sense of unity and national pride hadn't been experienced since the Coronation of Queen Elizabeth II in 1953. At last, in the face of the country's economic decline and grave employment problems, the people felt they had something to be proud of.

By dawn, July 29, there was hardly an inch of space to spare within a hundred yards of St. Paul's. By nine o'clock, when the first invited guests began to arrive, over a million people were crammed onto the sidewalks lining the route, complete with camping stoves, food, drinks for the children, and more than a few bottles of champagne to toast the happy couple.

Anyone who had feared a typically English rainy summer's day was happily proved wrong. From the moment the sun rose above the gray London streets, the day was radiant. A gentle breeze rippled through the trees in the royal parks and took the edge off the heat. The weather was perfect.

Diana awoke before six-thirty that morning—in her excitement she had hardly slept at all—and was taking a long bath at the Queen Mother's London home, Clarence House, where she had returned the previous day. She listened to the early-morning prewedding radio shows and peeped from behind curtains to see the thousands of people lining the Mall. For a moment, she was transfixed. It was awesome, she confided later to a girlfriend, to realize that *she*—who had been a mere teenager only twenty-eight days before—was the center of it all.

As soon as the television broadcasts started, Diana turned on the TV and switched from one channel to another, watching everything she could while consuming an enormous breakfast of orange juice, grapefruit, bacon and eggs, and toast and marmalade.

The first person in a procession of many to arrive at Clarence House was Kevin Shanley, Diana's hairdresser, who had brought with him three hair dryers ("just in case"), ten combs, and ten hairbrushes. He washed and blow-dried her hair, then styled it into the natural, informal style she preferred. When he finished, makeup artist Barbara Daly went to work, instructed by Diana to make her look as natural as possible; Charles disliked heavily made-up women. The makeup took forty-five minutes. The Emanuels arrived with the best-kept secret of all—the dress. Diana retired to her room with her sister Jane, who had come to help her dress. Together they watched the excited throngs lining the wedding route on the television set in the room. Diana was happy, wanting to get on with dressing and to get to the church.

But once she put on her magnificent gown and saw herself in the full-length mirror, she burst into tears. Jane ran to help her mop the tear stains and comfort her. Diana was uncontrollable. The other women in the room—maids, dressers, a lady-in-waiting, and a flower arranger—left so the sisters could be alone while Diana strove to master her emotions for the ordeal ahead. Half-sobbing, Diana told Jane, "All I want to do is marry Charles. I can't face all this . . . look at everyone . . . I can't go through with it."

But somehow she did.

Barbara Daly returned to repair the damage to the makeup, which was light, so the revisions took only a matter of minutes. However, Diana's eyes had to be bathed and redone.

Everyone agreed that the Emanuels' dress was a sensation: an elaborate, flowing creation of ivory silk paper taffeta, hand-embroidered with tiny mother-of-pearl sequins, with lace flounced sleeves, and a stunning, twenty-five-foot-long train, trimmed and edged with precious old lace. The huge crinoline skirt was puffed with one hundred yards of netting so that it billowed majestically. Forty-four yards of silk had been dyed ivory to suit Diana's complexion and to prevent its appearing a glaring white blob under the television lights. Diana's little bow, which had become her trademark in those early days, rested below the ruffled neckline on the boned bodice.

How deep the V of the neckline should go had been the subject of fierce debate. Diana had wanted a deep décolletage to reveal some flesh. The powers at Buckingham Palace decreed that since she was marrying the future head of the Church of England, her dress had to be particularly demure. As far as the world knew, Diana was one of the world's few surviving twenty-year-old virgins. In the end, there was a compromise: Diana persuaded the Emanuels to give her a deep V, but a froth of ruffles was added to temper the effect.

When Diana was finally dressed, David Emanuel sewed a last stitch in it, an age-old custom meant to bring luck. Clad in such a dress and wearing the Spencer diamond tiara and her mother's diamond earrings, Diana looked every inch a fairy princess. Inside, she was trembling like a leaf.

Slowly and nervously, she walked downstairs while a dozen people carried the train behind her and helped her into the glass coach that was to take her and her father to St. Paul's.

Prince Charles, too, had been wide awake that morning when Stephen Barry went to call him at seven. When Stephen turned on the radio, Charles listened to the prewedding program while he shaved, bathed, and dressed in a casual shirt and brown cords. He calmly ate a breakfast of grapefruit, fruit juice, and a boiled egg with toast. After all, all his life he had been prepared to cope with grand occasions, and this was no exception. After breakfast, Stephen began dressing the Prince in his naval uniform.

Charles wore the full dress uniform of a commander of Her Majesty's Royal Navy, together with a splendid blue sash that designated him a member of the ancient order of the Knights of the Garter. He looked magnificent. Fifteen minutes later, when he walked down the main stairs of the Grand Entrance of the palace—which cannot be seen from the Mall—all the members of the staff who were not going to St. Paul's stood at the bottom of the stairs and clapped. As he walked outside, the Prince shook hands with as many people as he could. "Thank you, thank you," he said warmly to each, before climbing into the coach with his brother Andrew for the journey to St. Paul's.

Andrew and their younger brother Edward would serve as Charles's "supporters," since he was not having a best man. Prince Andrew, as principal supporter, was responsible for the best man's traditional tasks, such as care of the wedding ring. The ring, which had been delivered to Buckingham Palace earlier that week, was made from the same piece of 22-carat Welsh gold as the wedding rings of the Queen, Queen Mother, Princess Margaret, and Princess Anne.

Inside the cathedral, the guests waited expectantly. Never before had such a distinguished collection of people been gathered together. Present were not only the entire British Royal Family and Diana's family, but also most of the crowned heads of Europe, monarchs from Africa, the Middle East, and Asia, 160 foreign presidents, prime ministers with their wives or husbands, politicians, civil servants, royal staff members, Diana's flatmates—who had front-row seats—and even the odd film star. Diana's divorced parents sat side by side in the front row, with their respective partners situated a discreet distance away.

Mrs. Nancy Reagan represented the President of the United States, who hadn't yet fully recovered from an assassination attempt four months earlier. Royal-wedding fever, in fact, seemed to have swept through the United States nearly as enthusiastically as it had in Britain. As ABC commentator Peter

Jennings explained, "It's the last of the royal spectacles. It's got color, sweep, music, occasion, and it's a great romantic story. It captures the imagination."

A thirty-minute peal of the giant bells known as Great Tom and Great Paul, accompanied by the twelve big bells in the northwest tower, heralded the event. As Diana stepped from her carriage, a barely audible sigh of admiration rippled through the onlookers.

As she marched up the red-carpeted steps of St. Paul's, Lady Sarah Armstrong-Jones and colleagues fought to control the river of ivory material flowing behind her. Inside the cathedral, David and Elizabeth Emanuel took over, adjusting her dress, her veil, her train, to be sure everything looked perfect for the grand entrance.

Diana had been given precisely three-and-a-half minutes to walk with her father, towing her train, up the long aisle of St. Paul's. The Lord Chamberlain and his staff pride themselves on clockwork efficiency and believe that strict timing is essential to achieve that.

Neither father nor daughter smiled as she approached Charles, while the congregation turned to watch the nervous bride. Diana appeared to be concentrating on making it to the altar ahead. She was most conscious of the need to support her father down the aisle, for there was serious doubt, at one point, that Earl Spencer, still suffering the effects of his stroke, was physically capable of giving the bride away. He went privately to St. Paul's a number of times to practice walking the distance and be sure he could manage it.

Afterward he said, "I was determined to walk Diana down the aisle, if it killed me. It was my duty, and I was not going to forgo it, if at all possible. But I must confess that far from me supporting Diana that day, she supported me. She was wonderful."

Diana heard the Archbishop of Canterbury tell the world:

"Here is the stuff of which fairy tales are made: the Prince and Princess on their wedding day. But fairy tales usually end at this point with the simple phrase 'They lived happily ever after.' This may be because fairy tales regard marriage as an anti-climax after the romance of courtship. This is not the Christian view. Our faith sees the wedding day not as the place of arrival but the place where the adventure really begins. Those who are married live happily ever after the wedding day if they persevere in the real adventure, which is the royal task of creating each other and creating a more loving world."

The Archbishop led the couple through the marriage ceremony. Apart from an endearingly nervous slip when she muddled Charles's names—thereby nearly marrying the Duke of Edinburgh!—the ceremony was faultless. Diana, in common with most modern brides but unlike previous royal brides, had opted to leave out the promise "to obey" her husband. Everyone in the cathedral noticed the wording "to love, honor, and cherish." Soon they would discover the reality of that oath.

As she took her wedding vows, Diana bade a final good-bye to the freedom she had known all her life—the freedom to do anything she wanted on the spur of the moment, to walk down a street alone, visit friends, go for a drive or to the cinema, have a private lunch in public or pop into a pub for a drink and a chat with a friend. Today, she was not simply marrying a man, but was embracing a job and all that it involved for the future. She had married a man for whom duty had and would always come first. And she, too, would soon discover that she had to feel as much commitment to the job, if not more, than to the man she was marrying.

At the end of the service, Diana looked relieved but still nervous as she and Charles walked up the aisle and out into the open air. A faint smile swept across her face when Charles spoke quietly to her, reassuring her, urging her to relax. The ordeal was over. They were married at last.

The Loving Lilliputians

The *New York Times*, February 11, 1863

In perhaps the first modern celebrity wedding, one of P. T. Barnum's most popular attractions, the thirty-one-inch General Tom Thumb, married Lavinia Bump with seemingly all New York craning for a look amidst avenue-closing pandemonium.

Marriage of General Tom Thumb and the Queen of Beauty
Who they are, what they have done, where they came from, where they are going
Their Courtship and wedding—Ceremonies, Presents, Crowds of people
The Reception—The Serenade

Those who did and those who did not attend the wedding of Gen. Thomas Thumb and Queen Lavinia Warren composed the population of this great Metropolis yesterday, and thenceforth religious and civil parties sink into comparative insignificance before this one arbitrating query of fate—Did you or did you not see Tom Thumb married? . . .

The marriage of Gen. Tom Thumb cannot be treated as an affair of no moment—in some respects it is most momentous. Next to Louis Napoleon, there is no one person better known by reputation to high and low, rich and poor, than he. . . .

Thumb was born, (so runs the legend,) of poor but honest parents on the fourth of February, 1838, in the pleasant burgh of Bridgeport, Conn. At his birth he weighed nine pounds and a half, so that he bid to become a bouncing boy. He grew steadily until he attained the age of eighteen months, when nature put a veto on his upward progress, and ordered him forever afterward to remain in *statu quo*. . . . He kept up his growing operations only 'till he had attained the height of thirty-one inches, and the weight of twenty-nine pounds. At the age of ten or thereabouts. Mr. Barnum, the Museumite found him out and brought him out, and has kept him out ever since. . . .

The Queen of beauty, Miss Lavinia Warren Bump, is a native of Middleboro, Massachusetts, where she was born on the thirty-first of October, 1842. She too is the child of ordinary sized persons, and has brothers and sisters of customary dimensions. She has, however, a little sister, Minnie Warren, who though sixteen years of age, is the smallest woman in the world. . . . The little queen, Lavinia, until she became one year old, grew as children generally do at that age, but from that time she increased in stature slowly, and ceased growing entirely when she was ten years of age. She attended school regularly, and found no difficulty in keeping up with the members of her classes. At home, her mother taught her to sew, knit, cook, and do all manner of housework . . . . She also has a knowledge of fancy work practiced by ladies who have the leisure to devote themselves to it. She is in a word, an accomplished lady—intelligent, pleasant, modest and agreeable. She is very lively in conversation, and speaks with all the confidence, and even wit of an accomplished and talented woman. She is fond of poetry, music, eloquence, and the fine arts generally; indeed, she is quite as charming mentally as she is physically. Her eye is bright, her smile sweet, her hair dark, and her figure perfection itself. . . . She was discovered by Mr. Barnum, and . . . engaged herself to him for a brief exhibition at the Museum.

While at Boston she was introduced to the general. She encountered her destiny—she met her "gray-eyed man." Tom, while gazing at her through the chill atmosphere of Boston alternately shivered and quivered. He literally fell desperately in love with her, and vowed his little vows, backed by the sternest of oaths. . . . The General and the Queen loved wisely, and after consulting with their mutual friend, protector and exhibitor, Mr. Barnum determined to do nothing rashly, but to submit the entire matter, with all due respect, to Mr. and Mrs. Bump. Inquiries concerning the "life" and character of Gen. T. Thumb met with favorable responses and the parental consent was given, the plighted troth was made, the ante-bridal preparations and the advancements of "only one week, only one week" were put forth. . . .

It was at first determined to make the affair strictly a private one, but the public desire was so great to see them that Mr. Barnum, who has kept modestly the back ground, was compelled to yield to the pressure. Bishop Potter, the venerable prelate who supervises the doings of the Episcopacy of this Diocese, was the clergyman selected for the performance of the ceremony. After a personal inspection of the Lilliputian pair the Bishop consented, and named Trinity Chapel as the place. Rev. Mr. Dix, recently appointed Rector of the Trinity Parish, didn't see the propriety of the Bishop's decree, and put down his foot, vetoing the use of the church for the purpose. Another church was recently found, and the arrangements for the wedding went smoothly on, until the Bishop discovered that there was "too much publicity given to the affair" and backed out from the agreement. . . .

The wedding took place yesterday, at twelve-and-one-half o'clock, in Grace Church on Broadway, the ceremony being performed by the Rev. Mr. Willey, of Bridgeport, Connecticut, assisted by the Rev. Dr. Taylor, of this City. . . . Long before the hour appointed for the ceremony a great concourse had gathered outside the church and that portion of Broadway between Union Square and ninth street was literally crowded, if not packed, with an eager and expectant populace. All classes of society were represented, not excluding the "spectacle man" and the woman retailer of apples. As the time approached for the ceremony of the nuptials, the crowd increased in density, every one exhibiting the most impatient desire to catch a glimpse at the happy pair when they should arrive. All the buildings in the vicinity of the church were made subservient to the general curiosity, and not a door, or window, or balcony which would in the least facilitate view, but was put into practical service. The smiling faces of the thousands of fair ladies thus assembled contributed not a little to the attractiveness and joyfulness of the occasion. The system of police was admirably executed. Order was preserved throughout the entire proceedings, and a general good feeling seemed to exist among the people. Stages and all vehicles excepting the carriages which contained invited guests and holders of tickets, were turned off Broadway at ninth street below the church, and at twelfth street above. In the intermediate space, and near each sidewalk, were stationed lines of policemen, who succeeded in maintaining their position until nearly noon, when the multitude became so vast that they were obliged to form new lines nearer the center of the street. The open space was then hardly of sufficient width to admit of the free passage of carriages, but the drivers threaded their way through, not withstanding the slight inconveniences which opposed them. To place a correct estimate upon the number of carriages that passed through the line, unless a person stood by and counted them one by one, would be impossible. There was one unbroken chain of them for over two hours preceding the arrival of the "little couple."

At twelve o'clock the carriage containing the bride and bridegroom; also Commodore Nutt and the sister of the bride, came rolling along very much to the relief of the outsiders. When the carriage had stopped, a general rush was made to get nearer it. Curiosity and excitement seemed to be unbounded for the time, and it was with the most strenuous exertions that the policemen could hold in check the determined and resolute crowd. . . .

The Church was comfortably filled by an audience comprising representatives of each and every strata of New York's respectable society. There were many elegantly dressed ladies and quite as many who paid but little respect either to the request of the inviter, the customary rules of etiquette, or the obvious proprieties of the occasion. It can hardly be considered the correct thing to newspaperize the presence of private individuals, however conspicuously placed or dressed, but the appearance of Maj. Gen. Burnside we may mention with propriety. The gallant soldier looked well and hearty, and received the evident regard of the audience with ease and dignity. There were but few reserved seats, the entire church edifice being open to the guests, with the exception of a few seats reserved for the bridal suite, and friends of the parties. . . .

At last they came. Preceding them was the self-possessed, the self-poised, the shrewd-eyed, kindly-faced Barnum — Barnum, the Prince of Showmen, the manager of the affair, which is, in his own word, "the biggest little thing that was ever known." After the General and the Queen, followed Com. Nutt, the groomsman, and Miss Minnie Warren, the bridesmaid. An instantaneous uprising ensued; all looked, few saw, many stood upon the seats, others stood upon stools placed on the seats; by many good breeding was forgotten, by very many the sanctity of the occasion and the sacredness of the ceremonies were entirely ignored. As the little party toddled up the aisle a sense of the ludicrous seemed to hit many, . . . [an] irrepressible and unpleasantly audible giggle ran through the church.

After a moment's reflection, the most absolute silence was maintained and the bride and groom, supported by the bridesmaid and groomsman, stood upon an elevated platform facing the altar, where stood the officiating ministers.

Tom Thumb looked cheerfully serene in full evening dress, his hair was curled and frizzled, his appearance that of a little old man in whom the juices of life were yet rich, and whose jolly days were not yet done.

Queen Lavinia appeared, soberly speaking, to great advantage. . . . Altogether she seemed exceedingly pretty, and her manner, like that of the General, was quiet, modest and proper. . . .

The service was performed in the usual manner, the responses being given by the happy pair in tones distinct and audible, without flush, flourish or nonsense. They were married as they should be and all things were done decently and in order.

The bride was given away by the Rev. Dr. Palmer, of Middleboro, with grace and dignity, and the gift was accepted by the gallant General, with every indication of grateful joy.

After the Benediction was pronounced, the General honestly kissed his wife, and in the presence of the entire audience bestowed upon her the "killing glance" with which he has, in days gone by, captivated so many millions of equally susceptible damsels. After a moments' tarrying, while Morgan's organ toiled out the delicious reminiscences of Mendelssohn's "Wedding March," they marched down the aisle arm in arm, and man and wife. . . .

The crowd outside remained patient at the expiration of which time the marriage ceremony was completed and Mr. and Mrs. Stratton—formerly Tom Thumb and Lavinia Warren—preceded by the bridemaid and brideman, again made their appearance to take the carriage. Another jam, another pressure and another stampede was the consequence. The former eagerness of the multitude was again manifest and did not even subside when the carriage had got several blocks off. It is not necessary to mention here of the shouts and yells and screeches with which the junior portion of the throng hailed the happy couple as they entered and left the church. Although it may seem ridiculous yet it is nevertheless true, that hundreds of persons, including adults, ran after the carriage not diminishing their speed until the Metropolitan Hotel had been reached. . . .

The sidewalks were crowded, and the windows of the buildings on each side were thronged. Policemen were detailed to preserve order in the vicinity of the hotel, as well as of the church. Vehicles were turned off the main thoroughfare at Houston and Spring streets, and the long line of carriages which was noticed at the church came pouring down toward the place of reception. The crowd followed, and in less than fifteen minutes the street in front of the hotel block was completely choked with human beings. . . .

The breath-expurgating, crinoline-crushing, bunion-pinching mass of conglomerated humanity that rushed eagerly to view other portions of the all absorbing ceremonies, likewise congregated at the bridal reception at the Metropolitan Hotel, the late residence of the Japanese Princes—the scene of the great Japanese ball—the ball of balls. Of course, the elite, the creme de la creme the upper ten, the bon ton, the select few—the very F.F.'s of the City—nay, of the country—together with many very many of what are called "citizens generally," found means of being present to view the Lilliputian welcome. . . .

Now, the General—by which we mean the happy bridegroom, Tom Thumb—or Charles Stratton Esq.,—while he is not celebrated as a Pascal, a Grotius, a Kirk White, a Colburn, or an Admirable Crichton—if he knows anything, knows what's what in a crowd. He—if anyone—can endure the flashing artillery of ten thousand eyes—the running fire of ten thousand comments—the bombardment of admiring exclamation, which the hero of such a scene must endure. He, therefore, looked not unusually astonished—nor remarkably surprised—but as pleased and joyful, and smiling and jolly as the happiest of happy bridesgrooms might, when he finally reached the Metropolitan Hotel, after the ceremony, and toddled through the crowd and climbed the stairs, gallantly helping up his bride, and keeping close at the heels of the sturdy M.P.'s, who portentously cleared the way. . . .

The weary minutes seemed hours while the tiny couple were making their toilettes, and in the meanwhile the main interest centered in the exhibition of bridal presents, which, vigilantly guarded by stout policemen, were to be seen in the Whilom reading room—now transformed into a gay and festive scene. The main attraction was, of course, the jewelry case, with the contributions from Ball & Black's, Tiffany's and others; the exquisite confectionery tower from Parkinson's caramel depot; the munificent bridal cake, with its delightful four cupids of quarterus; the gorgeous fruits and delicious wines in the cornucopia basket, from No. 585 Broadway; the fragrant bouquet from Geo. Brown, the neatly carved easy chair from 547 Broadway; the costly set of ermine from C. G. Gunther; the fans from Mrs. Cripps, and an incog. lady; the pair of slippers from Edwin Booth; the set of charms from August Belmont; the coral jewelry from J. A. Clark; the pearl ring from Mr. Mott; the locket and chain from Mrs. Belmont; the wonderful bird watch; the full tea set of five silver pieces lined with gold, from Mrs. James Gordon Bennett; the silver watch and cups from Mrs. Livingston and *ad libitum* silver spoons, castors, forks and pickers and napkin rings enough to make the newly married hummingbirds sing most discordant notes when the United States tax gatherer comes to collect the Government tax on plate. . . .

The buzz of conversation was soon hushed by the news which rapidly spread through the room—"They are coming," and there was a general rush to see the Brobdignagian bride and groom descend the stairs and proceed to the reception rooms. They . . . came tripping down the steps and melted like quicksilver through the yielding crowd, which rained down upon them a shower of compliments and a storm of searching glances. "Isn't she pretty?" "How graceful!" "How beautiful!" "How queenly!" "How matronly!" "How charming!" "Dear little creatures!" "Was there ever anything so lovely?" "Was there ever such a picture?" "Isn't it nice?" "What a manly bearing he has!" "Its like a fairy scene!" "Isn't it wonderful?" "Did you ever?" etc., etc. Amid all of which . . . the smiling twins—for such they seemed, were eventually guided to their pedestal—the piano—on which they were speedily raised by the athlete Dibble, and all was ready for . . . receiving the visitors with a nod, or a shake of the head, as the circumstances might prompt. The General and his lady had a smile and a bow for all, and manifested so much spirit, gaiety and life, that all were charmed beyond measure; in fact, Mr. and Mrs. Stratton acted as if they had been in the habit of being married.

At ten-and-one-half o'clock P.M., a band of music, consisting of eight pieces, congregated in front of the Metropolitan Hotel, and played "The Land of the Brave and the Home of the Free." About five hundred people were soon collected, and shortly afterward the Lilliputian pair appeared upon the balcony, to the great delight of the crowd below. When the music had been ceased, Gen. Thumb bowed his acknowledgment to the assemblage and said "Good night all." His bride then advanced and waved a kiss to the company, after which the bridal pair retired.

King of the Night

(an excerpt)

Laurence Leamer

One hundred and five years after Tom Thumb, Johnny Carson stepped into the Barnum role, invited Tiny Tim to wed his seventeen-year-old bride on The Tonight Show, and patented the electronic circus.

lthough Tiny Tim had already received his first national exposure on *The Merv Griffin Show*, it was the appearances with Johnny that made him famous. . . .

Johnny held up the cover of Tiny Tim's album *God Bless Tiny Tim,* and the record became one of the biggest hits of 1968. Tiny Tim was soon earning fifty thousand dollars a week or more. Johnny and *The Tonight Show* staff realized that they were riding a phenomenon. They booked him approximately every seven weeks, and every time he appeared he was a smash.

In September of the following year Tiny Tim used the hallowed platform of *The Tonight Show* to announce his engagement to seventeen-year-old Victoria May Budinger. Before the show Rudy Tellez says that he asked Tiny Tim, "what would happen if John asked you on the air to be married on the show?" According to Tellez, Tiny Tim replied "Ooohhoooohoooohooo."

Tiny Tim has a different recollection. "If someone came in beforehand, I don't remember," he says. "I would swear on a stack of telephone books, no way. Mr. Carson appreciated that he was the first to hear of our engagement. He paused for a while and he asked, 'Where are you going to get married and when?' I said, 'We're going to get married on Christmas Day in Haddonfield, New Jersey, in Miss Vicki's parents' house.'

"Mr. Carson thought for a few seconds. Then he said, 'Well, look, would you like to get married on our show? We'll do it in good taste. It will be like a night-time *Bride and Groom.*' I was familiar with that show. He said NBC would take care of the bills and pay for Miss Vicki's wedding gown. That was the key phrase. The only thing he said was, 'I can't do it on Christmas because I'll be away.' We both agreed on the seventeenth of December."

After saying yes to Johnny, Tiny began hearing unpleasant stories about his betrothed. "There were rumors when I met her and I was falling in love with her that a few days later she was making a play for the Christy Minstrels."

Tiny Tim had no quarrel with the New Christy Minstrels, but the rumors would have given a lesser man pause. Alas, once he said yes on *The Tonight Show*, the die was cast.

"If there was no Johnny Carson, there would have been no wedding," Tiny Tim says. "I always believed Miss Vicki did not love me. I told her mother after the Carson show was already set, 'Mrs. Budinger, Mrs. Budinger, I don't believe your daughter loves me. I believe that if your daughter saw me in '66 when I was nothing, she would have smiled and walked away. I believe she wants the marriage for herself. I know the way I am, I know my beliefs are strange, I don't believe in birth control.' Mrs. Budinger said, 'She wants to do it, and we'll see what the marriage will bring.'

"So I knew Miss Vicki didn't love me. And I myself was insecure. I proposed to three different girls when I was engaged to Miss Vicki. I would say to them, 'Let's run away.' Then I said no, I cannot break Miss Vicki's heart. And I would quickly call them up and say, 'I can't do that, I already promised Mr. Carson and I would break Miss Vicki's heart. She doesn't love me, but it would be a stigma on her future.' And so I went through with it."

Miss Vicki was not happy being married on *The Tonight Show*, either. She remembers telling her betrothed, "You better tell Mr. Carson you don't mean it, because I'm not going on television."

On December 17, 1969, the most-watched event in late-night television history took place: the marriage of Tiny Tim and Miss Vicki. There was no tougher ticket in New York than a place in the audience for *The Tonight Show* that evening.

Ed McMahon set the perfect tone for the evening, a blend of ersatz solemnity, merriment, and commerce: "We cordially request the pleasure of your company at the marriage of Tiny Tim and Miss Vicki right here on *The Tonight Show*. But right now here are some words of wisdom from Pepto-Bismol tablets."

Everything after the wedding would be anticlimactic. So Johnny stretched out the anticipation by talking first to his other guests, Phyllis Diller and Florence Henderson, who like Johnny had dressed formally for the evening. "And now here's the moment you've been waiting for," Johnny said finally. "A lot of people thought it wouldn't take place on this show."

Merrill Sindler, the set decorator, had spent three days designing and building a set that was supposed to be a Georgian English Church. The yellow curtain opened on an ornate blue building surrounded by thousands of yellow and white tulips. The door opened inward to reveal the wedding party. The men wore black coats, blue pants, and ruffled shirts, a campy fantasy of the eighteenth century. The women wore purple gowns with black bodices. Miss Vicki walked slowly forward, in a gown as white as innocence, her long veil pulled back to reveal brown bobbed hair curled as tightly as wood shavings. Tiny wore a long Victorian coat, his shoulder-length hair pressed and primped by a beauty consultant.

Tiny Tim vowed to be "sweet, gentle, kind, patient, not puffed up, charitable, slow to anger, and swift to forgive." When the ten-minute ceremony ended, the newlyweds walked over to *The Tonight Show* set.

"Congratulations, Tiny," Johnny said. "And Miss Vicki, you look just as pretty as brides always look. How do you feel, Tiny?"

"I feel great. I only hope and pray I can make Miss Vicki happy. I know I've been blessed with the most beautiful girl I've ever seen."

Tiny Tim thanked everyone. He thanked the owner of the Ground Floor restaurant, which was providing a free reception. He thanked the clothes designer for the free outfits. He thanked the hairdresser for the free stylings. He thanked the florist for the free flowers. He thanked the King's Inn in the Bahamas for the free honeymoon.

Tiny Tim and his bride drank natural honey and milk, while Johnny and the other guests toasted them with champagne. Then Tiny Tim sang a song that he had written for his bride:

> Oh won't you come and love me
> Oh pretty Vicki Mine,
> Oh won't you come and love me
> And be my valentine.

Later that evening the crowd at the reception was so enormous that Tiny Tim met only a few of the guests. The newlyweds had received scores of gifts, but they were stolen, hauled off like party favors. Tiny Tim was promised a videotape of the ceremony; even that he didn't receive.

C-40—Residence of Zane Grey, Avalon, Santa Catalina, California

9A-H413

A March down the Isle

Margo Kaufman

A small wedding should be the perfect way to avoid hullabaloo, expense and scheduling conflicts. Or maybe not. Kaufman suggests another route in this story from her collection, 1-800-Am-I-Nuts?

"There's no such thing as a small wedding," I warn Monica when she tells me she's getting married in May. Weddings follow a law of geometric progression: if you invite A, then you have to invite B and C; if you have just A, B, and C, you'll offend D, E, F, G, H, and I.

"But all we want is an intimate ceremony with our family and friends," Monica argues.

That was what my fiancé and I had wanted, too. "We can get married in our front yard," said Duke. "Or better still, on the beach." It sounded like a good plan. How difficult could it be?

Let me tell you.

"When's the wedding?" asked my sister the minute I called New York to tell her that Duke and I would no longer be living together on spec.

"I don't know yet," I stammered as my pulse began racing for the escape hatch. (Remarriage is an excellent test of just how amicable your divorce was.)

"You must set a date," Laurie ordered. "I want to get a cheap fare."

Duke and I decided January would be a good time for a wedding, mostly because it was the first available month that didn't include holidays, birthdays, or former wedding anniversaries.

"You must get married by the end of the year to file a joint tax return," my father decreed.

We decided Thanksgiving would be a better time for a wedding, mostly because we could cook a traditional turkey dinner ourselves and save the expense of a catered reception. But a head count of our parents, stepparents, siblings, their spouses, and their children revealed we were looking at a minimum guest list of fifty people — if we excluded all our friends.

"You must invite Duke's aunt and uncle," insisted my future mother-in-law, who had already invited them for me. "They live in Boston. They won't come."

But you can't rely on anyone not to come to a wedding, especially a wedding in Southern California. Within weeks, everyone we had ever met — long forgotten friends, ex-lovers, even college roommates — found out about our wedding, "wouldn't miss it for the world," and had, in fact, purchased nonrefundable plane tickets. I began to panic when I got a postcard from a friend in Tasmania.

"You must hire people to help you," exclaimed my future sister-in-law.

We decided to call a caterer. I discovered that we would have to pay fifteen hundred dollars for a turkey dinner and triple overtime for people to serve it because it was Thanksgiving. Duke sent me to check out a beachfront restaurant.

"You can sort of see the ocean from the dining room," I reported glumly. (My doubts were growing faster than the Homeless City of tents that blocked the view.) "And it's twenty dollars a person."

"I guess that's OK," Duke muttered morosely.

"Are you sure you want to go through with this?" I fretted as he ran out of the house to enjoy a few peaceful hours wandering the aisles of Pep Boys.

"I don't care," he snapped.

I didn't think it could get worse, but then it did get worse.

"You must ask Zara to be your flower girl," my future father-in-law informed me in front of his four-year-old granddaughter. (My brother's wife had already taken the liberty of buying her six-year-old daughter a dress.) Grandma called from Florida to threaten that my ailing grandfather would die if a rabbi didn't perform the ceremony.

"My wedding is turning into a pageant," I complained to my friend Lori.

"And it's not as if the British government is picking up the tab and I get to ride in a glass coach."

"Albert and I started out with six people and wound up with one hundred twenty-seven," she consoled me. "One of my cousins was seriously into alcohol. She drank all the white liquor and went to work on the brown. She ripped off the bottom of my wedding gown as I walked into the reception." I began to reminisce about the good old days when I was dating.

Duke was on the phone making inquiries about the price of a one-way ticket to Mexico City when I got home. "I'm canceling our wedding," I announced before he could read off his Visa number.

I haven't seen Duke so relieved since Magic Johnson flattened the Celtics in the championships with a miracle junior sky hook. "That's great, honey," he said. "Will you marry me?"

Curiously enough, everyone was more understanding about the wedding being canceled than they were about the wedding being held.

"Whatever makes you happy," said our friends and relatives, who effortlessly located doctors to attest to urgent inner-ear infections forbidding air travel, allowing refunds on their nonrefundable tickets.

So, Duke, an enormous bridal bouquet, and I took a boat to Santa Catalina Island. We checked into the Call of the Canyon Room at the Zane Grey Pueblo. Fern Whelan, the justice of the peace of the city of Avalon, agreed to marry us at five o'clock.

At noon Duke suggested we take a little hike up the airport road. The only hike I felt like taking was to the hairdresser, but I didn't want him to think he was marrying a poor sport. At three o'clock I was sunburned, weary from walking uphill, and too desperate to find a bathroom to marvel at the wild buffalo cow and calf that kept me from going behind a tree.

"Let's turn around," I said. "Just a little farther," Duke coaxed.

At four o'clock we were past Black Jack Mountain, some seven miles away. Duke suggested a shortcut back through the restricted area where hunters were shooting wild pigs.

I jumped in front of a speeding truck. "Stop!" I shrieked. "I'm late for my wedding."

All's well that ends well. We were married against a beautiful sunset on our terrace overlooking the harbor. The hotel graciously supplied champagne and a witness.

There is such a thing as a small wedding.

S Angel

Michael Chabon

*More than a half century after F.
Scott Fitzgerald described the Lost
Generation finding itself (see p. 31),
Michael Chabon brings a new group to
the party. Seemingly desperate to get lost,
Gen-X offers a novel twist on old love.*

(see p. 31)

On the morning of his cousin's wedding Ira performed his toilet, as he always did, with patience, hope, and a ruthless punctilio. He put on his Italian wool trousers, his silk shirt, his pink socks, to which he imputed a certain sexual felicity, and a slightly worn but still serviceable Willi Smith sport jacket. He shaved the delta of skin between his eyebrows and took a few extra minutes to clean out the inside of his car, a battered, faintly malodorous Japanese hatchback of no character whatever. Ira never went anywhere without expecting that when he arrived there he would meet the woman with whom he had been destined to fall in love. He drove across Los Angeles from Palms to Arcadia, where his cousin Sheila was being married in a synagogue Ira got lost trying to find. When he walked in late he disturbed the people sitting at the back of the shul, and his aunt Lillian, when he joined her, pinched his arm quite painfully. The congregation was dour and Conservative, and as the ceremony dragged on Ira found himself awash in a nostalgic tedium, and he fell to wishing for irretrievable things.

At the reception that followed, in the banquet room of the old El Imperio Hotel in Pasadena, he looked in vain for one of his more interesting young female cousins, such as Zipporah from Berkeley, who was six feet tall and on the women's crew at Cal, or that scary one, Leah Black, who had twice, in their childhoods, allowed Ira to see what he wanted to see. Both Ira and Sheila sprang from a rather disreputable branch of Wisemans, however, and her wedding was poorly attended by the family. All the people at Ira's table were of the groom's party, except for Ira's great-aunts, Lillian and Sophie, and Sophie's second husband, Mr. Lapidus.

"You need a new sport jacket," said Aunt Sophie.

"He needs a new *watch*," said Aunt Lillian.

Mr. Lapidus said that what Ira needed was a new barber. A lively discussion arose at table 17, as the older people began to complain about contemporary hairstyles, with Ira's itself—there was some fancy clipperwork involved—cited frequently as an instance of their inscrutability. Ira zoned out and ate three or four pounds of the salmon carpaccio with lemon cucumber and cilantro that the waiters kept bringing around, and also a substantial number of boletus-mushroom-and-goat-cheese profiteroles. He watched the orchestra members, particularly the suave-looking black tenor saxophonist with dreadlocks, and tried to imagine what they were thinking about as they blew all that corny cha-cha-cha. He watched Sheila and her new husband whispering and box-stepping, and undertook the same experiment. She seemed pleased enough—smiling and flushed and mad to be wearing that dazzling dress—but she didn't look like she was in love, as he imagined love to look. Her eye was restive, vaguely troubled, as though she were trying to remember exactly who this man was with his arms around her waist, tipping her backward on one leg and planting a kiss on her throat.

It was as he watched Sheila and Barry walk off the dance floor that the woman in the blue dress caught Ira's eye, then looked away. She was sitting with two other women, at a table under one of the giant palm trees that stood in pots all across the banquet room, which the hotel called the Oasis Room and had been decorated to suit. When Ira returned her gaze he felt a pleasant internal flush, as though he had just knocked back a shot of whiskey. The woman's expression verged a moment on nearsightedness before collapsing into a vaguely irritable scowl. Her hair was frizzy and tinted blond, her lips were thick and red but grim and disapproving, and her eyes, which might have been gray or brown, were painted to match her electric dress. Subsequent checking revealed that her body had aged better then her fading face, which nonetheless he found beautiful, and in which, in the skin at her throat and

MICHAEL CHABON　91

around her eyes, he thought he read strife and sad experience and a willingness to try her luck.

Ira stood and approached the woman, on the pretext of going over to the bar, a course which required that he pass her table. As he did so he stole another long look, and eavesdropped on an instant of her conversation. Her voice was soft and just a little woeful as she addressed the women beside her, saying something deprecating, it seemed to Ira, about lawyers' shoes. The holes in her earlobes were filled with simple gold posts. Ira swung like a comet past the table, trailing, as he supposed, a sparkling wake of lustfulness and Eau Sauvage, but she seemed not to notice him, and when he reached the bar he found, to his surprise, that he genuinely wanted a drink. His body was unpredictable and resourceful in malfunction, and he was not, as a result, much of a drinker; but it was an open bar, after all. He ordered a double shot of Sauza.

There were two men talking behind him, waiting for their drinks, and Ira edged a little closer to them, without turning around, so that he could hear better. He was a fourth-year drama student at UCLA and diligent about such valuable actorly exercises as eavesdropping, spying, and telling complicated lies to fellow passengers on airplanes.

"That Charlotte was a class A, top-of-the-line, capital B-I-T bitch," said one of the men, in the silky tones of an announcer on a classical music station. "And fucked up from her ass to her eyebrows." He had a very faint New York accent.

"Exactly, exactly," said the other, who sounded older, and well-accustomed to handing out obsequious counsel to young men. "No question. You had to fire her."

"I should have done it the day it happened. Ha ha. Pow, fired in her own bed."

"Exactly. Ha ha."

"Ira!" It was his cousin, the bride, bright and still pink from dancing. Sheila had long, kinky black hair, spectacular eyelashes, and a nose that, like Ira's, flirted dangerously, but on the whole successfully, with immenseness. He thought she looked really terrific, and he congratulated her wistfully. Ira and Sheila had at one time been close. Sheila hung an arm around his neck and kissed him on the cheek. Her breath blew warm in his ear. "What is that you're drinking?"

"Tequila," he said. He turned to try to get a glimpse of the men at the bar, but it was too late. They had been replaced by a couple of elderly women with empty highball glasses and giant clip-on earrings.

"Can I try?" She sipped at it and made a face. "I hope it makes you feel better than it tastes."

"It couldn't," Ira said, taking a more appreciative pull of his own.

Sheila studied his face, biting at her lip. They hadn't seen one another since the evening, over a year before, when she had taken him to see some dull and infuriating Soviet movie—*Shadow of Uzbek Love*, or something like that—at UCLA. She was looking, it seemed to him, for signs of change.

"So are you dating anyone?" she said, and there was a glint of tension in her casual tone.

"Lots of people."

"Uh huh. Do you want to meet someone?"

"No thanks." Things had gotten a little wiggly, Ira now recalled, in the car on the way home from Westwood that night. Sheila drove one of those tiny Italian two-seaters capable of filling very rapidly with sexual tension, in particular at a stop light, with Marvin Gaye coming over the radio and a pretty cousin in the driver's seat, chewing thoughtfully on a strand of hair. Ira, in a sort of art-house funk, had soon found himself babbling on about Marx and George Orwell and McCarthyism, and praying for green lights; and when they arrived at his place he had dashed up the steps into his apartment and locked the door behind him. He shook his head, wondering at this demureness, and drained the glass of tequila. He said, "Do you want to dance?"

They went out onto the floor and spun around a few times slowly to "I'll Never Be the Same." Sheila felt at once soft and starchy in her taffeta dress, gigantic and light as down.

"I really wish you would meet my friend Carmen," said Sheila. "She needs to meet a nice man. She lives next door to my parents in Altadena. Her husband used to beat her but now they're divorced. She has the most beautiful gray eyes."

At this Ira stiffened, and he blew the count.

"Sitting right over there under the palm tree? In the blue dress?"

"Ouch! That's my foot."

"Sorry."

"So you noticed her! Great. Go on, I., ask her to dance. She's so lonesome anymore."

The information that the older woman might actually welcome his overtures put him off, and somehow made him less certain of success. Ira tried to formulate a plausible excuse.

"She looks mean," he said. "She gave me a nasty look not five minutes ago. Oh, hey. It's Donna."

"Donna!"

Donna Furman, in a sharp gray sharkskin suit, approached and kissed the bride, first on the hand with the ring, then once on each cheek, in a gesture that struck Ira as oddly papal and totally Hollywood. Donna started to tell Sheila how beautiful she looked, but then some people with cameras came by and swept Sheila away, so Donna threw out her arms to Ira, and the cousins embraced. She wore her short hair slicked back with something that had an ozone smell and it crackled against Ira's ear. Donna was a very distant relation, and several years older than Ira, but as the Furmans had lived in Glassell Park, not far from Ira's family in Mt. Washington, Ira had known Donna all his life, and he was glad to see her.

This feeling of gladness was not entirely justified by recent history, as Donna, a girl with a clever tongue and a scheming imagination, had grown into a charming but unreliable woman, and if Ira stopped to consider he might, at first, have had a bone or two to pick with his fourth cousin once removed. She was a good-looking, dark-complected lesbian—way out in the open about all that—with a big bust and a twelve-thousand-dollar smile. The vein of roguery that had found its purest expression in Sheila's grandfather, Milton Wiseman, a manufacturer of diet powders and placebo aphrodisiacs, ran thin but rich through Donna's character. She talked fast and took recondite drugs and told funny stories about famous people whom she claimed to know. Despite the fact that she worked for one of the big talent agencies in Culver City, in their music division, and made ten times what Ira did waiting tables and working summers at a Jewish drama camp up in Idyllwild, Donna nonetheless owed Ira, at the time of this fond embrace, three hundred and twenty-five dollars.

"We ought to go out to Santa Anita tonight," Donna said, winking one of her moist brown eyes, which she had inherited from her mother, a concentration camp survivor, a Hollywood costume designer, and a very sweet lady who had taken an overdose of sleeping pills when Donna was still a teenager. Donna's round, sorrowful eyes made it impossible to doubt that somewhere deep within her lay a wise and tormented soul; in her line of work they were her trump card.

"I'd love to," said Ira. "You can stake me three hundred and twenty-five bucks."

"Oh, right! I forgot about that!" Donna said, squeezing Ira's hand. "I have my checkbook in the car."

"I heard you brought a date, Donna," Ira went on, not wanting to bring out the squirreliness in his cousin right off the bat. When Donna began to squeeze your hand it was generally a portent of fictions and false rationales. She was big on touching, which was all right with Ira. He liked being touched. "So where is the unfortunate girl?"

"Over there," Donna said, inclining her head toward Ira as though what she was about to say were inside information capable of toppling a regime or piling up a fortune in a single afternoon. "At that table under the palm tree, there. With those other two women. The tall one in the flowery thing, with the pointy nose. Her name's Audrey."

"Does she work with you?" said Ira, happy to have an excuse to stare openly at Carmen, seated to the right of Donna's date and now looking back at Ira in a way that, he thought, could hardly be mistaken. He wiggled his toes a few times within his lucky pink socks. Donna's date, Audrey, waved her fingers at them. She was pretty, with an expensive, blunt hairdo and blue eyes, although her nose was as pointed as a marionette's.

"She lives in my building. Audrey's at the top, at the very summit, I., of a *vast* vitamin pyramid. Like, we're talking, I don't know, ten thousand people, from Oxnard to Norco. Here, I'll take you over." She took hold of the sleeve of Ira's jacket, then noticed the empty shot glass in his hand. "Hold on, let me buy you a drink." This was said without a trace of irony. "Drinking shots?"

"Sauza. Two story."

"A C.C. and water with a twist and a double Sauza," she said to the bartender. "Tequila makes you unlucky with women."

"See that blonde Audrey is sitting beside?"

"Yeah? With the nasty mouth?'

"I'd like to be unlucky with her."

"Drink this," said Donna, handing Ira a shot glass filled to the brim with liquid the very hue of hangover and remorse. "From what I heard she's a basket case, I. Bad husband. A big mess. She keeps taking these beta-carotene tablets every time she has a Seven and Seven, like it's some kind of post-divorce diet or I don't know."

"I think she likes me." They had started toward the table but stopped now to convene a hasty parley on the dance floor, beneath the frond of a squat fan palm. Donna had been giving Ira sexual advice since he was nine.

"How old are you now, twenty-one?"

"Almost."

"She's older than I am, Ira!" Donna patted herself on the chest. "You don't want to get involved with someone so old. You want someone who still has all her delusions intact, or whatever."

Ira studied Carmen as his cousin spoke, sensing the truth in what she said. He had yet to fall in love to the degree that he felt he was capable of falling, had never written villanelles or declarations veiled in careful metaphor, nor sold his blood plasma to buy champagne or jonquils, nor haunted a mailbox or a phone booth or a certain café, nor screamed his beloved's name in the streets at three in the morning, heedless of the neighbors, and it seemed possible that to fall for a woman who had been around the block a few times might be to rob himself of much of the purely ornamental elements, the swags and antimacassars of first love. No doubt Carmen had had enough of such things. And yet it was her look of disillusion, of detachment, those stoical blue eyes in the middle of that lovely, beaten face, that most attracted him. It would be wrong to love her, he could see that; but he believed that every great love was in some measure a terrible mistake.

"Just introduce me to her, Donnie," he said, "and you don't have to pay me back."

"Pay you back what?" said Donna, lighting up her halogen smile.

She *was* a basket case. The terra cotta ashtray before her on the table, stamped with the words EL IMPERIO, was choked with the slender butts of her cigarettes, and the lit square she held in her long, pretty fingers was trembling noticeably and spewing a huge, nervous chaos of smoke. Her gray eyes were large and moist and pink as though she had been crying not five minutes ago, and when Donna, introducing Ira, laid a hand on her shoulder, it looked as though Carmen might start in again, from the shock and the unexpected softness of this touch. All of these might have escaped Ira's notice or been otherwise explained, but on the empty seat beside her, where Ira hoped to install himself, sat her handbag, unfastened and gaping, and one glimpse of it was enough to convince Ira that Carmen was a woman out of control. Amid a blizzard of wadded florets of Kleenex, enough to decorate a small parade float, Ira spotted a miniature bottle of airline gin, a plastic bag of jellybeans (all black ones), two unidentifiable vials of prescription medication, a crumpled and torn road map, the wreckage of a Hershey bar, and a key chain, in the shape of a brontosaurus, with one sad key on it. The map was bent and misfolded in such a way that only the fragmentary words S ANGEL, in one corner, were legible.

"Carmen Wallace, this is my adorable little cousin Ira," Donna said, using the hand that was not resting on Carmen's bare shoulder to pull at Ira's cheek. "He asked to meet you."

"How do you do," said Ira, blushing badly.

"Hi," Carmen said, setting her cigarette on the indented lip of the ashtray and extending the tips of her fingers toward Ira, who paused a moment—channeling all of his sexual energy into the center of his right palm—then took them. They were soft and gone in an instant, withdrawn as though he had burned her.

"And this is Audrey—"

"Hi, Audrey."

"—and Doreen, who's a—friend?—of the groom's."

Ira shook hands with these two and, once Carmen had moved her appalling purse onto the floor beside her to make room for him, soon found himself in the enviable position of being the only man at a table of five. Doreen was wearing a bright yellow dress with an extremely open bodice; she had come to her friend Barry's wedding exposing such a great deal of her remarkable chest that Ira

wondered about her motives. She was otherwise a little on the plain side and she had a sour, horsey laugh, but she was in real estate and Donna and Audrey, who were thinking of buying a house together, seemed to have a lot to say to her. There was nothing for him and Carmen to do but speak to each other.

"Sheila says you live next door to her folks?" Ira said. Carmen nodded, then turned her head to exhale a long jet of smoke. The contact of their eyes was brief but he thought it had something to it. There was about an inch and a half of Sauza left in Ira's glass and he drained a quarter inch of it, figuring this left him with enough to get through another five questions. He could already tell that talking to Carmen was not going to be easy, but he considered this an excellent omen. Easy flirtation had always struck him as an end in itself and one which did not particularly interest him.

"Is it that big wooden house with the sort of, I don't know, those *things*, those rafters or whatever, sticking out from under all the roofs?" He spread the fingers of one hand and slid them under the other until they protruded, making a crude approximation of the overhanging eaves of a California bungalow. There was such a grand old house, to the north of Sheila's parents, that he'd always admired.

Another nod. She had a habit of opening her eyes very wide, every so often, almost a tic, and Ira wondered if her contact lenses might not be slipping.

"It's a Hetrick and Dewitt," she said bitterly, as though this were the most withering pair of epithets that could be applied to a house. These were the first words she had addressed to him and in them, though he didn't know what she was talking about, he sensed a story. He took another little sip of tequila and nodded agreeably.

"You live in a Hetrick and Dewitt?" said Doreen, interrupting her conversation with Donna and Audrey to reach across Audrey's lap and tap Carmen on the arm. She looked amazed. "Which one?'

"It's the big pretentious one on Orange Blossom, in Altadena," Carmen said, stubbing out her cigarette. She gave a very caustic sigh and then rose to her feet; she was taller than Ira had thought. Having risen to her feet rather dramatically, she now seemed uncertain of what to do next and stood wavering a little on her blue spike heels. It was clear she felt that she had been wrong to come to Sheila's wedding, but that was all she seemed able to manage, and after a moment she sank slowly back into her seat. Ira felt very sorry for her and tried to think of something she could do besides sit and look miserable. At that moment the band launched into "Night and Day," and Ira happened to look toward the table were he had left his aunts. Mr. Lapidus was pulling out his aunt Sophie's chair and taking her arm. They were going to dance.

"Carmen, would you like to dance?" Ira said, blushing, and wiggling his toes.

Her reply was no more than a whisper, and Ira wasn't sure if he heard it correctly, but it seemed to him that she said, "Anything."

They walked, separately, out onto the dance floor, and turned to face each other. For an awful moment they just stood, tapping their hesitant feet. But the two old people were describing a slow arc in Ira's general direction, and finally in order to forestall any embarrassing exhortations from Mr. Lapidus, who was known for such things, Ira reached out and took Carmen by the waist and palm, and twirled her off across the wide parquet floor of the Oasis Room. It was an old-fashioned sort of tune and there was no question of their dancing to it any way but in each other's arms.

"You're good at this," Carmen said, smiling for the first time that he could remember.

"Thanks," said Ira. He was in fact a competent dancer—his mother, preparing him for a fantastic and outmoded destiny, had taught him a handful of hokey old steps. Carmen danced beautifully, and he saw to his delight that he had somehow hit upon the precise activity to bring her, for the moment anyway, out of her beta-carotene and black jellybean gloom. "So are you."

"I used to work at the Arthur Murray on La Cienega," she said, moving one hand a little lower on his back. "That was fifteen years ago."

This apparently wistful thought seemed to revive her accustomed gloominess a little, and she took on the faraway, hollow expression of a taxi dancer, and grew heavy in his arms. The action of her legs became overly thoughtful and accurate. Ira searched for something to talk about, to distract her with, but all of the questions that came up with had to do, at least in some respect, with *her*, and he sensed that anything on this subject might plunge her, despite her easy two-step, into an irrevocable sadness. At last the bubble of silence between them grew too great, and Ira pierced it helplessly.

"Where did you grow up?' he said, looking away as he spoke.

"In hotels," said Carmen, and that was that. "I don't think Sheila is happy, do you?" She coughed, and then the song came abruptly to an end. The bandleader set down his trumpet, tugged the microphone up to his mouth, and announced that in just a few short moments the cake was going to be cut.

When they returned to the table a tall, handsome man, his black hair thinning but his chin cleft and his eyes pale green, was standing behind Carmen's empty chair, leaning against it and talking to Donna, Audrey, and Doreen. He wore a fancy, European-cut worsted suit, a purple and sky blue paisley necktie, a blazing white-on-white shirt, and a tiny sparkler in the lobe of his left ear. His nose was large, bigger even than Ira's, and a complex shape, like the blade of some highly specialized tool; it dominated his face in a way that made the man himself seem dominating. The shining fabric of his suit jacket caught and stretched across the muscles of his shoulders. When Carmen approached her place at the table, he drew her chair for her. She thanked him with a happy and astonishingly carnal smile, and as she sat down he peered, with a polished audacity that made Ira wince in envy, into the scooped neck of her dress.

"Carmen, Ira," said Doreen, "this is Jeff Freebone." As Doreen introduced the handsome Mr. Freebone, all of the skin that was visible across her body colored a rich blood-orange red. Ira's hand vanished momentarily into a tanned, forehand-smashing grip. Ira looked at Donna, hoping to see at least some hint of unimpressedness in her lesbian and often cynical gaze, but his cousin had the same shining-eyed sort of *Tiger Beat* expression on her face as Doreen and Carmen—and Audrey, for that matter—and Ira realized that Jeff Freebone must be very, very rich.

"What's up Ira?" he said, in a smooth, flattened-out baritone to which there clung a faint tang of New York City, and Ira recognized him, with a start, as the coarse man at the bar who had fired an unfortunate woman named Charlotte in her own bed.

"Jeff here used to work in the same office as Barry and me," Doreen told Carmen. "Now he has his own company."

"Freebone Properties," Carmen said, looking more animated than she had all afternoon. "I've seen the signs on front lawns, right?"

"Billboards," said Donna. "Ads on TV."

"How was the wedding?" Jeff wanted to know. He went around Carmen and sat down in the chair beside her, leaving Ira to stand, off to one side, glowering at his cousin Donna, who was clearly going to leave him high and dry in this. "Did they stand under that tent thing and break the mirror or whatever?"

Ira was momentarily surprised, and gratified, by this display of ignorance, since he had taken Jeff for Jewish. Then he remembered that many of Donna's Hollywood friends spoke with a shmoozing accent whether they were Jewish or not, even ex-cheerleaders from Ames, Iowa, and men named Lars.

"It was weird," Carmen declared, without elaborating—not even Jeff

Freebone, apparently, could draw her out—and the degree of acquiescence this judgment received at the table shocked Ira. He turned to seek out Sheila among the hundreds of faces that filled the Oasis Room, to see if she was all right, but could not find her. There was a small crowd gathered around the cathedral cake at the far end of the room, but the bride did not seem to be among them. Weird—what had been weird about it? Was Sheila not, after all, in love with her two hours' husband? Ira tapped his foot to the music, self-conscious, and pretended to continue his search for Sheila, although in truth he was not looking at anything anymore. He was mortified by the quickness with which his love affair with the sad and beautiful woman of his dreams had been derailed, and all at once—the tequila he had drunk had begun to betray him—he came face to face with the distinct possibility that not only would he never find the one he was meant to find, but that no else ever did, either. The discussion around the table hurtled off into the imaginary and vertiginous world of real estate. Finally he had to take hold of a nearby chair and sit down.

"I can get you three mil for it, sight unseen," Jeff Freebone was declaring. He leaned back in his seat and folded his hands behind his head.

"It's worth way more," said Donna, giving Carmen a poke in the ribs. "It's a work of art, Jeff."

"It's a Hetrick and Dewitt," said everyone at the table, all at once.

"You have to see it," Doreen said.

"All right then, let's see it. I drove my Rover, we can all fit. Take me to see it." There was a moment of hesitation, during which the four women seemed to consider the dictates of decorum and the possible implications of the proposed expedition to see the house that Carmen hated.

"The cake is always like sliced cardboard at these things, anyway," said Donna.

This seemed to decide them, and there followed a general scraping of chairs and gathering of summer wraps.

"Aren't you coming?" said Donna, leaning over Ira—who had settled into a miserable, comfortable slouch—and whispering into his ear. The others were already making their way out of the Oasis Room. Ira scowled at her.

"Hey, come on, I. She needs a realtor, not a lover. Besides, she was way too old for you." She put her arms around his neck and kissed the top of his head. "Okay, sulk. I'll call you." Then she buttoned her sharkskin jacket and turned on one heel.

After Ira had been sitting alone at the table for several minutes, half hoping his aunt Lillian would notice his distress and bring over a piece of cake or a petit four and a plateful of her comforting platitudes, he noticed that Carmen, not too surprisingly, had left her handbag behind. He got up from his chair and went to pick it up. For a moment he peered into it, aroused, despite himself, by the intimacy of this act, like reading a woman's diary, or putting one's hand inside her empty shoe. Then he remembered his disappointment and his anger, and his fist closed around one of the vials of pills, which he quickly slipped into his pocket.

"Ira, have you seen Sheila?"

Ira dropped the purse, and whirled around. It was indeed his aunt Lillian but she looked very distracted and didn't seem aware of having caught Ira in the act. She kept tugging at the fringes of her wildly patterned scarf.

"Not recently," said Ira. "Why?"

Aunt Lillian explained that someone, having drunk too much, had fallen onto the train of Sheila's gown and torn it slightly; this had seemed to upset Sheila a good deal and she had gone off somewhere, no one knew where. The bathrooms and the lobbies of the hotel had all been checked. The cake-cutting was fifteen minutes overdue.

"I'll find her," said Ira.

He went out into the high, cool lobby and crossed it several times, his heels clattering across the marble floors and his soles susurrant along the Persian carpets. He climbed a massive oak staircase to the mezzanine, where he passed through a pair of French doors that opened onto a long balcony overlooking the sparkling pool. Here he found her, dropped in one corner of the terrace like a blown flower. She had taken the garland from her brow and was twirling it around and around in front of her face with the mopey fascination of a child. When she felt Ira's presence she turned, and seeing him, broke out in a teary-eyed grin that he found very difficult to bear. He walked over to her and sat down beside her on the rough stucco deck of the balcony.

"Hi," he said.

"Are they all going nuts down there?"

"I guess. I heard about your dress. I'm really sorry."

"It's all right." She stared through the posts of the balustrade at the great red sun going down over Santa Monica. There had been a lot of rain the past few days and the air was heartbreakingly clear. "You just feel like such a, I don't know, a big stupid puppet or something, getting pulled around."

Ira edged a little closer to his cousin and she laid her head against his shoulder, and sighed. The contact of her body was so welcome and unsurprising that it frightened him, and he began to fidget with the vial in his pocket.

"What's that?" she said, at the faint rattle.

He withdrew the little bottle and held it up to the dying light. There was no label of any kind on its side.

"I sort of stole them from your friend Carmen."

Sheila managed an offhand smile.

"Oh—how did that work out? I saw you dancing."

"She wasn't for me," said Ira. He unscrewed the cap and tipped the vial into his hand. There were only two pills left, small, pink, shaped like commas—two little pink teardrops. "Any idea what these are? Could they be beta-carotene?"

Sheila shook her head and extended one hand, palm upward. At first Ira thought she wanted him to place one of the pills upon it, but she shook her head again; when he took her outstretched fingers in his she nodded.

"Ira," she said in the heaviest of voices, bringing her bridal mouth toward his. Just before he kissed her he closed his eyes, brought his own hand to his mouth, and swallowed, hard.

"My darling," he said.

The Bride, 1839–1840

(an excerpt)

Queen Victoria

Queen Victoria comes last, an unexpected romantic figure. As she details her courtship and marriage to Albert—essentially handpicked by her advisers—she proves that love can overcome even the most unlikely circumstances.

109

Journal
18 April 1839

Lord M. then said, 'Now, Ma'am, for this other matter.' I felt terrified (foolishly) when it came to the point; too silly of me to be frightened in talking to him. Well, I mustered up courage, and said that my Uncle's great wish— was—that I should marry my cousin Albert—who was with Stockmar—and that I thought Stockmar might have told him (Ld. M.) so; Lord M. said, No— Stockmar had never mentioned a word; but, that I had said to my Uncle, I could decide nothing until I saw him again. 'That's the only way,' said Lord M. . . .

12 July 1839

Talked of my Cousins Ernest and Albert coming over,—my having no great wish to see Albert, as the whole subject was an odious one, and one which I hated to decide about; there was no engagement between us, I said, but that the young man was aware that there was the possibility of such a union; I said it wasn't right to keep him on, and not right to decide before they came; and Lord M. said I should make them distinctly understand anyhow that I couldn't do anything for a year. . . .

10 October 1839

As we were returning along the new walk, one of my pages came running with a letter from Uncle Leopold, saying my cousins would be here very soon;

they sent on the letter announcing their arrival. I said to Lord M. I was sure they would come this day, but he would never believe it. At ½ p. 7 I went to the top of the staircase and received my 2 dear cousins Ernest and Albert,—whom I found grown and changed, and embellished. It was with some emotion that I beheld Albert—who is beautiful. I embraced them both and took them to Mamma; having no clothes they couldn't appear at dinner . . . Talked [to Lord Melbourne] of my cousins' bad passage; their not appearing on account of their *négligé,* which Lord M. thought they ought to have done, at dinner and certainly after. 'I don't know what's the dress I would appear in, if I was allowed,' said Lord M., which made us laugh.

After dinner my Cousins came in, in spite of their *négligé,* and I presented them to Lord Melbourne. I sat on the sofa with Lord Melbourne sitting near me, and Ernest near us and Albert opposite — (he is so handsome and pleasing), and several of the ladies and gentlemen round the sofa. I asked Lord M. if he thought Albert like me, which he is thought (and which is an immense compliment to me). 'Oh! yes, he is,' said Lord M., 'it struck me at once.'

11 October 1839
Albert really is quite charming, and so excessively handsome, such beautiful blue eyes, an exquisite nose, and such a pretty mouth with delicate moustachios and slight but very slight whiskers; a beautiful figure, broad in the shoulders and a fine waist; my heart is quite going . . . It is quite a pleasure to look at Albert when he gallops and valses, he does it so beautifully, holds himself so well with that beautiful figure of his. . . .

13 October 1839
Talked of my cousins having gone to Frogmore; the length of their stay being left to me; and I said seeing them had a good deal changed my opinion (as to

marrying), and that I must decide soon, which was a difficult thing. 'You would take another week,' said Lord M.; 'certainly a very fine young man, very good-looking,' in which I most readily agreed, and said he was so amiable and good tempered, and that I had such a bad temper; of my being the 1st now to own the advantage of beauty, which Lord M. said smiling he had told me was not to be despised, in spite of what I had said to him about it. Talked of my cousins being religious. 'That strong Protestant feeling is a good thing in this country,' he said, 'if it isn't intolerant,'—which I assured him it was not. I had great fun with my dear cousins after dinner. I sat on the sofa with dearest Albert; Lord Melbourne sitting near me, Ernest playing at chess, and many being seated round the table . . . Eos [Prince Albert's greyhound] came in again and yawned. I played 2 games at Tactics with dear Albert, and 2 at Fox and Geese. Stayed up till 20 m. p. 11. A delightful evening.

14 October 1839

After a little pause I said to Lord M., that I had made up my mind (about marrying dearest Albert).—'You have?' he said; 'well then, about the time?' Not for a year, I thought; which he said was too long; that Parliament must be assembled in order to make a provision for him, and that if it was settled 'it shouldn't be talked about,' said Lord M.; 'it prevents any objection, though I don't think there'll be much; on the contrary,' he continued with tears in his eyes, 'I think it'll be very well received; for I hear there is an anxiety now that it should be; and I'm very glad of it; I think it is a very good thing, and you'll be much more comfortable; for a woman cannot stand alone for long, in whatever situation she is' . . . Then I asked, if I hadn't better tell Albert of my decision soon, in which Lord M. agreed. How? I asked, for that in general such things were done the other way,—which made Lord M. laugh. When we got up, I took Lord M.'s hand, and said he was always so kind to me,—which he has always been; he was so kind, so fatherly about all this. I felt very happy . . . Talked to Lord Melbourne after dinner of my hearing Albert couldn't sleep these last few days; nor I either, I added; that he asked a good deal about England, about which I tried to give him the most agreeable idea.

15 October 1839
At about ½ p. 12 I sent for Albert; he came to the Closet where I was alone, and after a few minutes I said to him, that I thought he must be aware why I wished [him] to come here, and that it would make me too happy if he would consent to what I wished (to marry me); we embraced each other over and over again, and he was so kind, so affectionate; Oh! to feel I was, and am, loved by such an Angel as Albert was too great delight to describe! he is perfection; perfection in every way—in beauty—in everything! I told him I was quite unworthy of him and kissed his dear hand—he said he would be very happy [to share his life with her] and was so kind and seemed so happy, that I really felt it was the happiest brightest moment in my life, which made up for all I had suffered and endured. Oh! how I adore and love him, I cannot say!! how I will strive to make him feel as little as possible the great sacrifice he has made; I told him it was a great sacrifice,—which he wouldn't allow . . . I feel the happiest of human beings. . . .

19 October 1839
My dearest Albert came to me at 10 m. to 12 and stayed with me till 20 m. p. 1. Such a pleasant happy time. He looked over my shoulder and watched me writing to the Duchess of Northumberland, and to the Duchess of Sutherland; and he scraped out some mistakes I had made. I told him I felt so grateful to him and would do everything to make him happy. I gave him a ring with the date of the ever dear to me 15th engraved in it. I also gave him a little seal I used to wear. I asked if he would let me have a little of his dear hair. . . .

27 October 1839

I signed some papers and warrants etc. and he [Prince Albert] was so kind as to dry them with blotting paper for me. We talked a good deal together, and he clasped me so tenderly in his arms, and kissed me again and again . . . and was so affectionate, so full of love! Oh! what happiness is this! How I do adore him!! I kissed his dear hand. He embraced me again so tenderly.

1 November 1839

At 7 m. p. 6 came my most beloved Albert and stayed with me till 10 m. p. 7 . . . He was so affectionate, so kind, so dear, we kissed each other again and again . . . Oh! what too sweet delightful moments are these!! Oh! how blessed, how happy I am to think he is *really* mine; I can scarcely believe myself so blessed. I kissed his dear hand, and do feel so grateful to him; he is such an angel, such a very great angel! — We sit so nicely side by side on that little blue sofa; no two Lovers could ever be happier than we are! . . . He took my hands in his, and said my hands were so little he could hardly believe they were hands, as he had hitherto only been accustomed to handle hands like Ernest's.

10 November 1839

I sat on the sofa with Albert and we played at that game of letters, out of which you are to make words, and we had great fun about them. Albert gave 'Pleasure,' and when I said to the people who were puzzling it out, it was a very common word Albert said, But not a very common thing, upon which Lord M. said, 'Is it truth, or honesty?' which made us all laugh.

14 November 1839

We kissed each other so often, and I leant on that dear soft cheek, fresh and pink like a rose . . . It was ten o'clock and it was the time for his going . . . I gave Albert a last kiss, and saw him get into the carriage and—drive off. I cried much, felt wretched, yet happy to think that we should meet again soon! Oh! how I love him, how intensely, how devotedly, how ardently! I cried and felt so sad. Wrote my journal. Walked. Cried. . . .

5 December 1839

Talked of where she [her mother] was to go to, and her living in a hired house, Lord M. thought it would not be well looked upon etc.; and I got eager and dreaded she would make all this a pretext to stay in the house etc. . . . Talked of my horror at being married in the Chapel Royal . . . I complained that everything was always made so uncomfortable for Kings and Queens, and it was making this odious etc.—He looked ill and said he was unwell. . . .

7 February 1840

We were seated as usual, Lord Melbourne sitting near me. Talked . . . of the Marriage Ceremony; my being a little agitated and nervous; 'Most natural,' Lord M. replied warmly; 'how could it be otherwise?' Lord M. was so warm, so kind, and so affectionate, the whole evening, and so much touched in speaking of me and my affairs. Talked of my former resolution of never marrying. 'Depend upon it, it's right to marry,' he said earnestly; 'if ever there was a situation that formed an exception, it was yours; it's in human nature, it's natural to marry; the other is a very unnatural state of things; it's a great change—it has its inconveniences: everybody does their best, and depend upon it you've done well; difficulties may arise from it,' as they do of course from everything.

8 February 1840

At ½ p. 4 the Carriage and Escort appeared, drove through the center gate, and up to the door; I stood at the very door; 1st stepped out Ernest, then Uncle Ernest, and then Albert, looking beautiful and so well; I embraced him and took him by the hand and led him up to my room; Mamma, Uncle Ernest, and Ernest following. I sat on the sofa with my beloved Albert, Lord Melbourne sitting near me . . . Lord M. admired the diamond Garter which Albert had on, and said 'Very handsome.' I told him it was my gift; I also gave him (all before dinner) a diamond star I had worn, and badge. Lord M. made us laugh excessively about his new Coat, which he said, 'I expect it to be the thing most observed.'

On the morning of their wedding, which took place in the Chapel Royal, St. James's, the Queen sent a note by hand to the Prince:

10 February 1840
How are you today, and have you slept well? I have rested very well, and feel very comfortable today. What weather! I believe, however, the rain will cease.

Send one word when you, my most dearly loved bridegroom, will be ready. Thy ever-faithful, Victoria R.

Journal
10 February 1840
Got up at a ¼ to 9 — well, and having slept well; and breakfasted at ½ p. 9. Mamma came before and brought me a Nosegay of orange flowers. My dearest kindest Lehzen gave me a dear little ring . . . Had my hair dressed and the wreath of orange flowers put on. Saw Albert for the last time alone, as my Bridegroom.

Saw Uncle, and Ernest whom dearest Albert brought up. At ½ p. 12 I set off, dearest Albert having gone before. I wore a white satin gown with a very deep flounce of Honiton lace, imitation of old. I wore my Turkish diamond necklace and earrings, and Albert's beautiful sapphire brooch. Mamma and the Duchess of Sutherland went in the carriage with me. I never saw such crowds of people as there were in the Park, and they cheered most enthusiastically. When I arrived at St. James's, I went into the dressing-room where my 12 young Train-bearers were, dressed all in white with white roses, which had a beautiful effect. Here I waited a little till dearest Albert's Procession had moved into the Chapel. I then went with my Train-bearers and ladies into the Throne-room, where the Procession formed; . . . the Procession looked beautiful going downstairs. Part of the Color Court was also covered in and full of people who were very civil. The Flourish of Trumpets ceased as I entered the Chapel, and the organ began to play, which had a beautiful effect. At the Altar, to my right, stood Albert.

The Ceremony was very imposing, and fine and simple, and I think ought to make an everlasting impression on every one who promises at the Altar to keep what he or she promises. Dearest Albert repeated everything very distinctly. I felt so happy when the ring was put on, and by Albert. As soon as the Service was over, the Procession returned as it came, with the exception that my beloved Albert led me out. The applause was very great, in the Color Court as we came through; Lord Melbourne, good man, was very much affected during the Ceremony and at the applause . . . I then returned to Buckingham Palace alone with Albert; they cheered us really most warmly and heartily; the crowd was immense; and the Hall at Buckingham Palace was full of people; they cheered us again and again . . . I went and sat on the sofa in my dressing-room with Albert; and we talked together there from 10 m. to 2 till 20 m. p. 2. Then we went downstairs where all the Company was assembled and went into the dining-room—dearest Albert leading me in . . . Talked to all after the breakfast, and to Lord Melbourne, whose fine coat I praised.

I went upstairs and undressed and put on a white silk gown trimmed with swansdown, and a bonnet with orange flowers. Albert went downstairs and undressed. At 20 m. to 4 Lord Melbourne came to me and stayed with me till 10 m. to 4. I shook hands with him and he kissed my hand. Talked of how well everything went off. 'Nothing could have gone off better,' he said, and of the people being in such good humor . . . I begged him not to go to the party; he was a little tired; I would let him know when we arrived; I pressed his hand once more, and he said, 'God bless you, Ma'am,' most kindly, and with such a kind look. Dearest Albert came up and fetched me downstairs, where we took leave of Mamma and drove off at near 4; I and Albert alone.

As soon as we arrived [at Windsor] we went to our rooms; my large dressing room is our sitting room; the 3 little blue rooms are his . . . After looking about our rooms for a little while, I went and changed my gown, and then came back to his small sitting room where dearest Albert was sitting and playing; he had put on his windsor coat; he took me on his knee, and kissed me and was so dear and kind. We had our dinner in our sitting room; but I had such a sick headache that I could eat nothing, and was obliged to lie down in the middle blue room for the remainder of the evening, on the sofa, but, ill or not, I never, never spent such an evening . . . He called me names of tenderness, I have never yet heard used to me before—was bliss beyond belief! Oh! this was the happiest day of my life!—May God help me to do my duty as I ought and be worthy of such blessings.

11 February 1840

When day dawned (for we did not sleep much) and I beheld that beautiful angelic face by my side, it was more than I can express! He does look so beautiful in his shirt only, with his beautiful throat seen. We got up at ¼ p. 8. When I had laced I went to dearest Albert's room, and we breakfasted together. He had a black velvet jacket on, without any neckcloth on, and looked more beautiful than it is possible for me to say . . . At 12 I walked out with my precious Angel, all alone—so delightful, on the Terrace and new Walk, arm in arm! Eos our only companion. We talked a great deal together. We came home at one, and had luncheon soon after. Poor dear Albert felt sick and uncomfortable, and lay down in my room . . . He looked so dear, lying there and dozing. . . .

12 February 1840
Already the 2nd day since our marriage; his love and gentleness is beyond everything, and to kiss that dear soft cheek, to press my lips to his, is heavenly bliss. I feel a purer more unearthly feel than I ever did. Oh! was ever woman so blessed as I am.

13 February 1840
My dearest Albert put on my stockings for me. I went in and saw him shave; a great delight for me.

acknowledgments

Excerpts from *Madame Bovary* by Gustave Flaubert, translated by Lowell Bair, translation copyright © 1959 by Bantam, a division of Bantam Doubleday Dell Publishing Group, Inc. Used by permission of Bantam Books, a division of Bantam Doubleday Dell Publishing Group, Inc. ✳ Excerpt from *Plaza Suite* by Neil Simon, copyright © 1969 by Neil Simon. Reprinted by permission of Random House, Inc. ✳ For excerpts from *Lives of the Saints*, permission granted by International Creative Management, Inc., copyright © 1984 by Nancy Lemann. ✳ "The Bridal Party" reprinted with the permission of Scribner, a Division of Simon & Schuster, from *The Short Stories of F. Scott Fitzgerald*, edited by Matthew J. Bruccoli. Copyright 1930 by the Curtis Publishing Company. Copyright renewed © 1958 by Frances Scott Fitzgerald Lanahan. ✳ Excerpt from *Diana: A Princess and Her Troubled Marriage* by Nicholas Davies. Copyright © 1992 by Nicholas Davies. Published by arrangement with Carol Publishing Group. A Birch Lane Press Book. ✳ Excerpt from *King of the Night* by Laurence Leamer, copyright © 1989 Leda Productions, Inc. ✳ "A March down the Isle" from *1-800-AM-I-NUTS?* by Margo Kaufman, copyright © 1982 by Margo Kaufman. Reprinted by permission of Random House, Inc. ✳ Text of "S Angel" from *A Model World and Other Stories* by Michael Chabon. Copyright © 1991 by Michael Chabon. By permission of William Morrow and Company, Inc. ✳ Excerpt from *Queen Victoria in Her Letters and Journals* by Christopher Hibbert. Copyright © 1984 by Christopher Hibbert. Used by permission of Viking Penguin, a division of Penguin Books USA Inc.

photographs

Photographs on title page and page 2 courtesy of Maria Fernandez. ✳ Photograph on page vi copyright © Edward Keating; photographs on pages 20, 63 and 88 copyright © Edward Keating/*The New York Times*. ✳ Photograph on page 10 copyright © 1996 by Paramount Pictures Corporation. Courtesy of Photofest. ✳ Photographs on pages 30 and 66 courtesy of The New-York City Historical Society. ✳ Photographs on pages 42 and 108 courtesy of Marvin Langley. ✳ Photograph on page 54 courtesy of British Information Services. ✳ Photograph on page 76 courtesy of Photofest.* ✳ Postcard on page 82 courtesy of Margo Kaufman.* ✳ Photograph on page 99 copyright © Richard Canavan.

additional thanks to...

Larry Peterson for negotiating rights and permissions, and for finding Tiny Tim; Maria Fernandez for her image research; Rachel Florman for help with production; Morgan Entrekin for a second chance, and Colin Dickerman for his patient support; Jennifer Lyons for making it happen; and finally, Deborah Foley for cooperation above and beyond the call.

*Copyright holder, if any, unknown. Those with information, please contact Balliett & Fitzgerald, Inc. via the publisher.